Catechism of Musical Aesthetics

Hugo Riemann
Translated by H. Bewerunge

CAMBRIDGE UNIVERSITY PRESS

Cambridge, New York, Melbourne, Madrid, Cape Town,
Singapore, São Paolo, Delhi, Mexico City

Published in the United States of America by Cambridge University Press, New York

www.cambridge.org
Information on this title: www.cambridge.org/9781108057301

© in this compilation Cambridge University Press 2013

This edition first published 1895
This digitally printed version 2013

ISBN 978-1-108-05730-1 Paperback

This book reproduces the text of the original edition. The content and language reflect the beliefs, practices and terminology of their time, and have not been updated.

Cambridge University Press wishes to make clear that the book, unless originally published by Cambridge, is not being republished by, in association or collaboration with, or with the endorsement or approval of, the original publisher or its successors in title.

AUGENER'S EDITION No. 9207.

CATECHISM

OF

MUSICAL AESTHETICS.

BY

DR. H. RIEMANN.

TRANSLATED BY

THE REV. H. BEWERUNGE,
PROFESSOR OF ECCLESIASTICAL MUSIC, MAYNOOTH COLLEGE.

AUGENER & CO., LONDON:
86 NEWGATE STREET, E.C., I FOUBERT'S PLACE & 81 REGENT STREET, W.

PRINTED IN GERMANY.

PREFACE.

More than thirty years ago Hanslick's work "Vom Musikalisch-Schönen"[*] put an end to the previous vague rhetorical declamation on the essence and object of music, and stimulated to keener reflection on the different factors which combine to produce that effect which music produces. Since then a pretty extensive literature has arisen, one portion of which retains Hanslick's system of Formalism — that is to say, declares the form of music to be its substance —, while the other maintains that music is capable of rendering poetic ideas musically, and that that is its office, and rejects all music that will be merely music, as an empty play with forms. To these two groups, which until within a recent period were the only ones existing, of late a third one seems to be added which, in a certain sense, reconciles the contradicting views of the other two, not simply by way of compensation and compromise, but by giving a third definition which combines and materially perfects the other two.

I became acquainted with those books, with whose positive results the following pages fairly coincide, only after I had written and partly delivered these lectures; I do not, however, regret this, because they undoubtedly would have influenced my train of thought,

---

[*] Translated by G. Cohen and published by Novello under the title "The Beautiful in Music".

and hindered me from finding something, though it may be but little, that is new, and that gives to my work the stamp of individuality. When Fr. von Hausegger says that music is first and above all *expression*, and when Arthur Seidl lays stress on *"entering, with one's feeling, into the forms of movement of music,"* that, certainly, is something akin to the *Subjectivation* of music on which I insist. Still I believe that by distinguishing the *elementary*, which arises simply from the impulse to *impart* oneself (Hausegger's "Music as Expression"), from the *formal,* which belongs to the impulse to *play* (which according to Hanslick is everything), and from the *characteristic*, which in itself is alien to music and is drawn into its sphere only by the impulse to *imitate* (music not as the expression of the subject but as expression of an imagined object) — I have set up something that is worth developing. For the listener there result principally two altogether different ways of perceiving music, in one of which music is felt as the manifestation of one's own *will* (complete subjectivation), while in the other it is, partly at least, objectivated by the *imagination*. But the more, in absolute music, the formal preponderates over the elementary, that is to say, the less music is felt, and the more it is made — the more imperfectly shall we subjectivate it, the more it will remain outside of us; on the other hand, imitative music, in spite of scene and programme, — if only it does not proceed too restlessly, but rather leaves time for the expression of sentiment of the represented beings to develop (that is to assume form) — can affect us so sympathetically that, for moments at least, we can completely subjectivate it and identify ourselves with the object represented.

H. R.

I.

Elementary Factors:
Pitch of Tone, Strength of Tone, Manner of Movement.

"Music is in its expression universally *intelligible*, not only to the *musician*, but to men in general. Nor is music essentially different in the *folk-song* and the *Bach fugue* or the *Beethoven symphony*. Though the complicated character of a work of art may render it hard to be understood, yet the same means, which when taken separately are intelligible to all, are used in the largest as well as in the smallest composition; music speaks to us in a language the words and grammar of which we need not first learn . . . What is musically inadmissible is so not because it is contrary to a rule established by the musician, but because it is contrary to a natural law imposed on the musician by his *human* sentiment — because it is logically untrue and self-contradictory".

By means of this pertinent remark of Moritz Hauptmann ("Natur der Harmonik und der Metrik", pp. 6—7) I would wish, first of all, to remove the suspicion that the subject of the following investigations belongs to the "professional" study of music.* On the contrary, we shall keep altogether aloof from what is technical in music, in its theoretical as well as its practical bearing — that is to say, with regard to the mathematical, physical, and

---

* Even more precisely Lazarus says (Das Leben der Seele, II, p. 323): "Psychology in laying down a principle explaining the actual effect of a musical piece, is not justified in confining itself to skilled musicians and taking no notice of more than nine tenths of those who listen to the piece."

psychological foundation of the rules of composition as well as their management in composition, and the correct exposition of the intention of the composer in reproduction, in the performance — and shall give, in a form intelligible to every educated person, a concise explanation of the means which music generally employs to produce its effects. For the reply to the question "How do we hear Music?" demands, in the first instance, an explanation of the various means of musical art, that we may, then, be able to determine how our ear, our heart, our intellect, acts in reference to them.

The question concerning the *object* of music does not occupy us in the following pages. We shall have an opportunity, later on, of seeing that the object for which a certain piece of music is conceived, can and must, indeed, exercise an essential influence on its construction as well as on the opinion formed of it by the hearer. But this object lies outside music itself. The question as to an object of music at all appears an idle one; "as the bird sings, that dwells amid the boughs", thus man sings and makes music from an *inward* necessity; the artist creates from an inward creative impulse, following the innate desire to impart and to play. To create is to him an enjoyment, to impart a necessity. So soon as he creates for a definite object, a part of the ideal freedom of the artist is lost, though we cannot deny that this loss may be counterbalanced by the inspiring loftiness of the proposed object.

On the other hand we shall be occupied, and indeed quite specially, almost exclusively, with the question of the *capability* of music — the question what music *can do*, what it *effects*, and what are the various *means* by which it produces its effects. But the investigation of these means should not be looked upon as undertaken in the interest of their practical application, but rather as arising from the natural desire to understand how, on the one hand, the musical work of art is produced in the mind of its creator, and how, on the other, the artistic effect upon the hearer necessarily follows.

The first answer, and that which, without reflection, would be given by everyone, to the question concerning the means by which music produces its artistic effects, is: *The Tone* — also called sound or note — or, to express it quite generally: the *audible*. For even though, in the present state of musical development, the composer can, without the aid of actual sound, write down the grandest musical works in characters intelligible to the musician; though Beethoven wrote his last symphonies and his *Missa Solemnis* when his sense of hearing was entirely gone; and though a capable musician is able to understand and enjoy a musical work of art by simply reading it: still, in both cases the *objective* sounds are only represented by *subjectively imagined* ones, just as analogous mental images of the visible world are familiar to everyone, and must be present with the utmost vividness in the mind of the imitative artist, if he is to create successfully. To whatever intensity and distinctness this inward sight and hearing may be brought, the imagined form and the imagined tone are ever but the substitutes of the imagination for the actually visible and actually audible.* The question whether, as Plato says, the image conceived by the artist, the *Idea*, be not the prior and more perfect thing, and what appears to the senses, only an earthly and imperfect imitation of it, shall be left untouched: The idea eludes our investigation; we are not concerned even with the notation of the musical work, which, under circumstances, may be nearer to the idea than the audible performance — our object is mainly and solely the *audible* musical work of art.

To everything audible one property attaches which may be called *musical*, and is often so called: we need only think of human speech, in which, indeed, we shall

---

* Ed. Grell alludes to this in his "Gutachten über die Musikalische Kompositions-Schule der Kgl. Akademie der Künste" (Ges. Aufsätze und Gutachten, p. 65): "What the pupil works out and brings to his teacher, is neither for himself, nor for the teacher real, living music . . . . With the draughtsman the written notation — the drawing — is the thing itself." A direct reproduction of the mental image on the part of the musician is given only in the improvisation, the fantasia, which, however, is distinguished from the finished picture by the fact that the artist has no time to reflect and alter. We see the two arts are so fundamentally different, that conclusions cannot be drawn from the one for the other. If the teacher has not enough imagination to hear distinctly the written composition by simply reading it, or if he thinks the pupil has imagined it as sounding differently from what it really does, there is only one rational method to remedy that for the future: the work must be made to sound, by being performed.

find even highly developed musical qualities, or of the song of the birds, the howling of the wind, the rolling of the thunder, the creaking of the mill wheel. That many a musical idea has actually been evoked by this music of nature, is a well known fact; and it is equally notorious, that music likes to draw the idealised imitation of such noises into the sphere of its representations.

There are two things that seem to constitute the essence of the tone, and in which, accordingly, we have to recognize more special resources of music, namely *pitch* and *strength* of tone — or rather, in as much as both exist, in the inarticulate sounds of nature, mostly in a fluctuating condition — the *rising and falling of the tone* and the *increase and decrease of the tone*. Where such constant transition is absent and sounds of different pitch follow each other so that they can easily be distinguished, or where stronger impulses mark different moments of time, as, for instance, in the hoof-beats of a galloping horse, or in the sound of the smith's hammer or of the cooper's mallet, a third quality of sounds manifests itself, namely the *quickness of movement* showing itself in their succession. But also in the rising and falling as well as in the increase and decrease of the tone the effect of *quickness of change* that takes place, can be observed.

If anywhere, then in music, the proposition of Heraclitos holds good that everything is in constant motion (πάντα ῥεῖ). For even the single tone, whose pitch does not vary and whose strength remains the same, is well known to be the result of a constant motion in regular periodic form, of vibrations of an elastic body propagated in the air. Each single vibration, of which the higher notes accomplish many thousands in the second, is as it were a prototype of the form which underlies even the greatest productions of art — rest, movement, and return to rest. The departure from the state of equilibrium corresponds to a violent tension, to excitement; and the return from this to the former is equivalent to the reverse, to relaxation, to a calming down. But in reality we are not at all conscious of this continual change of tension and relaxation, of the vibrating body; the tone which remains at the same pitch and strength rather appears to us as something steady and at rest. It is only the *change* of pitch or strength that produces the impression of *movement*; and, in particular, rising pitch and increasing strength appear to us as *positive*, that is to say, as developing, progressing, advancing movement, while falling pitch and decreasing strength appear as *negative*, that is to say, as backward, retrogressive movement. In an analogous manner *increase of quickness* in sequence of tones of recognisable difference in pitch or strength, awakens the idea of intensification, that is to say, appears as positive form of movement, while *lessening of speed* appears as the negative form.

If in the first place we look more closely at the changes of pitch, we see easily that in them the essence of *melody* consists. It is not, however, the different positions of the single sounds that constitute this essence of melody; but it is rather the *actual raising and lowering of pitch*, the *transition* from lower to higher tones, or the reverse, that produces the aesthetic effect. The root principle, therefore, of melody is the *continuous* change of pitch, not the graduated change. Though, in spite of this, there does not, and cannot, exist any melody which consists only in continual alteration of pitch, in continued sliding up and down, as when the storm howls, or when one passes a finger along a vibrating string, this proves nothing against the correctness of the above definition. It only proves that, besides increase and decrease of pitch, other factors contribute to produce the aesthetic impression of music.

This rising and falling of pitch *appears* to be continous even when it is graduated. Of the correctness of this paradoxical statement we can convince ourselves by producing the notes of a melody not in close connection, *legato*, but interrupted by rests, *staccato*. Then only is obtained the special impression of a graduated progression, but at the same time that of a *stilted* gait, of the dainty lifting and setting down of the little feet, the *tripping*, and, with a vague line of melody, that of *groping* and *fumbling*. Similar to this is the impression made when a violin-player attacks every tone with great precision, as it is the mannerism of some *virtuosi* who strive to produce a great volume of sound; the effect produced thereby is that of *firmness*, while the warmth and liveliness of the playing lose considerably. We come, therefore, to the conclusion that the separate definite tones are to be regarded as pausing upon a certain pitch for the purpose of comparison, or control, of the degree of increase or diminution, and that the *legato* transition from one pitch to another appears not as a skip, but as *a continous increase or decrease executed rapidly.*

That, finally, even a *staccato* melody, if only it really appears as the movement of a single part, is to be understood in the *sense* of a continuous raising and lowering of pitch, certainly seems still more paradoxical, but is just as true. For in the *staccato* execution we have always the impression of leaping over the space of the continuous line of tone that lies between the separate notes.

Perhaps, besides the possibility of swelling or diminishing the strength of the tone at pleasure, the most important factor of the warmth, liveliness, and heartiness of tone in stringed instruments, as well as in the human voice, is the fact that, in the transitions from one pitch to another, they can really produce a continuous increase or decrease; the *Portamento*, accordingly, is the most concrete embodiment of the melodious principle, in so far as it is the audible transition from one pitch to another in a continuous line. But for the same reason, a frequent use of the *Portamento* — as also of the chromatic scale, which is closely akin to it — is rather naturalistic. Further on (II) we shall have to examine more closely that principle which restricts melody and makes it dependant essentially on the imagination, namely harmony, under whose spell the melodic progression is idealised to graduated, not continuous, change of pitch, while the really continuous transition remains only as a product of our imagination, which understands the sequence of separate tones as continuous, alike in instruments in which the continuous increase is possible — as in the human voice and stringed instruments — and in those where it is impossible — namely in all instruments with fixed intonation.

After the precedent set by Newton many attempts have been made to draw a parallel between tones and colours, and, misled by the old mysticism of the number seven, writers have tried to establish a connection between the seven degrees of the scale and the seven colours of the rainbow. They have gone even further and attempted, after the analogy of musical harmonies, by copying the proportions of the numbers of vibrations, to compose colour harmonies; thus first the inventor of the "colour piano", Louis Bertrand Castel (1739), and even in most recent times Fr. W. Unger in a paper in Poggendorff's

"Annalen" and in his work "Die bildende Kunst" (Göttingen 1858), also the aesthetic writer Zimmermann, and even Helmholtz. According to them red-yellow-blue would be a major colour chord, orange-green-violet a minor colour chord. But there have not been wanting thorough investigators who repudiate this parallel. Thus E. Brücke, in his "Physiologie der Farben für die Zwecke der Kunstgewerbe" (Leipzig 1866), does not consider a universal law for the aesthetic effect of combinations of colours as warranted, and also the philosopher Herrmann Lotze, who, as a critic, has hardly been surpassed, in his "Geschichte der Aesthetik in Deutschland" (Munich 1868), takes up a position of absolute scepticism towards the doctrine of colour harmonies. He rightly emphasizes that "two colours like red and blue are incomparably more different than two tones ever can be" (p. 290). In making this statement he undoubtedly thinks in the first instance of two tones at the interval which the colour-harmonists assume for red and blue, that is, the interval of a fifth. If he had extended his view beyond the octave, and left out of consideration the scale of seven colour tones, which, after all, is only a fiction, he would have recognised a different analogy between the effects of colours and of tones, one in which the whole range of tone, from the lowest depths to the loftiests heights, comes into comparison with the spectrum.

The colours only with a certain minimum rate of vibration come across the threshold of perceptibility, and withdraw themselves again from perception as soon as they exceed a maximum rate of vibration. It is well known that dark red is the slowest, violet the quickest of colours, and beyond either of them the colours cease to be perceptible. Between the two terminals, however, there is evidently a continuous transition from red towards yellow, green, and blue, and the supposition of a limited number of definite colours is more or less arbitrary.

A very similar thing must be said about pitch of tone. The range of tone is limited below as well as above. Vibrations that are too slow (less than about 16 in the second), and those that are too quick (more than 40,000 in the second) elude our perception. And in the transition from the lowest depth to the loftiest height we can right well verify differences of impression similar to those that various colours produce. The analogy is not quite perfect in as far as the very highest tones are clearly in the strongest contrast to the very lowest ones, while, strange to say, the quickest colours, in their effect on our feelings, again approach the slowest ones, both appearing as the darker colours. By a common musical feeling the principal colours of this musical spectrum, extending through about eleven and a half octaves, are called by the principal classes of the human voice: Bass, Tenor, Alto (Contralto), and Soprano (Treble), although these four together comprise only the four middle octaves. In addition to these we have the intermediate colours Barytone (between Bass and Tenor) and Mezzo-Soprano (between Alto and Soprano). A certain instinctive comprehension of such a parallelism between colours and regions of tone is shown, for instance, by the fact that for a long time it has been usual to make red the colour of the Soprano, yellow the colour of the Tenor, green the colour of the Alto, and blue the colour of the bass, whenever it is required to mark the voices of the singers by means of coloured rosettes, or the part-books by coloured labels. Bass and Tenor, then, on the one hand, Alto and Soprano on the other hand, receive complementary colours, and the pitch of the voices is only apparently in contradiction to the order of the colours in the spectrum, because the characteristic notes of the Tenor are not the middle ones of its compass, but the high ones, and similarly the characteristic notes of the Alto are not the middle ones, but the low ones.

We have seen that change of pitch, the rising and falling, appear as movement, either positive or negative, as increase or decrease, — that is to say, as *quantitative* change, as augmentation or diminution of the living power. On the other hand, tones of different pitch, if there is no transition from one to the other, but each is considered by itself, whether they are in succession or simultaneous, appear as *qualitatively* different, just like the colours, in which, too, we do not perceive the varying quickness of vibration. This probably is the consequence of the fact that, in determining pitch, two kinds of quantitative distinctions stand in reciprocal relation to each other. The higher the tone, the quicker the vibrations, but the smaller the moving mass; the length of the sound-wave always stands in inverse ratio to the number of vibrations in the same time. Justly, therefore, Lotze says (loc. cit. p. 272):

"Gradation, of some kind, indeed, is to be found as well in the rising pitch of the sounding tones as in the increasing number of sound-waves; but the increase of pitch implies no impression of a growing number such as is to be predicated of the sound waves. The rising pitch rather gives instead of that something quite peculiar, a gradation that we might call an increase of qualitative intensity, an increase of liveliness. In addition to this we have to consider another point. In proportion to its increasing pitch and apart from its strength, the higher tone is perceived as thinner, sharper, acuter, the lower one as broader and blunter. Perhaps this peculiarity depends on the shorter duration of each wave in the higher tones, through which a greater rate of repetition in the same time becomes possible .... Apart from its strength, therefore, each tone, each apparent *activity from within*, on account of its qualitative nature, has a measurable value of greater or less liveliness. But in two directions this activity consumes itself; it becomes impossible, and the tone disappears from the range of the audible, when its liveliness, its pitch, increases continually; for then the body from which this life should go forth, becomes, as it were, attenuated down to nothing; but it disappears also, when, in the lowest degrees of the scale, the breadth and mass of the audible crushes the liveliness. *Thus the highest tones resemble a movement of ever increasing velocity and ever decreasing size of the thing moved; the lowest ones resemble an ever slackening speed of a mass growing without limit.*"

From this it is very easily intelligible how, contrary to the usual acceptation the falling of pitch may occasionally appear as positive form of movement, and the rising as negative. What asserts itself then is, in the former case, not the decreasing velocity, but the growing mass; in the latter, not increasing velocity but the diminishing mass. Such a contrary effect regularly takes place whenever the *falling* is combined with a *crescendo*, or the *rising* with a *diminuendo*. Gust. Engel ("Aesthetik der Tonkunst", p. 48) says: "In the lower regions of tone strength has the character of the massive, in the higher ones that of the intense". He does not, however, seem to me to be on the right track when he continues: "The natural seat of the *crescendo* is to be found from the lower tones to the middle ones and from the higher ones to the middle ones, that of the *decrescendo* in the reverse order." Perhaps the contrary would be more correct? Engel arrives at his conclusion by the observation that the lowest and the highest tones are weak, a statement with which I unfortunately cannot agree. If a thirty two foot C on the organ does not speak easily, that has its own reasons (large supply of wind); but I cannot possibly admit that the tones of a contrabass tuba are weak as compared, say, with those of a horn or a trumpet, or that the piccolo flute is weaker than the clarionet. And with this premise the conclusion also falls.

From the compensating co-operation of the two factors indicated, namely, the mass and the velocity of the moving thing, we get an explanation of the peculiar differences of aesthetic value between high and low tones, which though somewhat in contradiction to the wider acceptation of the word, we may call the *colour* of the tone. The general usage of language, calling tones that are produced by slower vibrations and longer sound-waves, *low* and *dark*, and those produced by quicker vibrations and shorter sound-waves, *high* and *clear*, actually designates that different quality in the sense of a different effect of light: the high notes are clear, that is to say, exposed to more light, the low ones are dark, that is to say, more hidden from the light. True, we have here again in the first instance essentially the quantitative distinction of more or less of light; and, in fact, we had to admit above that the scale of tones, unlike the scale of colours, does not, in the highest pitch, return to the effect of more darkness, but goes on advancing towards more brightness, we might say, becomes an intolerably bright white, which has a dazzling effect and thereby also does away with the possibility of discriminating.

If, for the present, we retain this conception of the different pitch as a difference of colour, which in the lowest depths vanishes into black and in the highest ascents into white, still we have explained only a part of the effect of a single tone, even if we leave its strength as yet out of the question. For another peculiar quality attaches to every tone according to the instrument by which it is produced. There only we arrive at what is *commonly* called tone colour, — what Helmholtz, for instance, means by the term. Whether one and the same tone, — say the once-marked c, — is sounded by a 'cello or a violin, a bassoon or a flute, a male or female voice, makes a great difference in its aesthetic effect. Produced by a 'cello, bassoon, or a Tenor or Bass voice, it will sound high and clear; produced by a violin, flute, or female voice it will sound low and dark. Moreover it will sound differently again according as it is produced by a 'cello *or* bassoon *or* a male voice, and similarly with the others. Even the 'cello itself can give the same c a different colour by a different kind of bowing, and with the singer, apart from the special quality of his organ, the different manner of attack, the vocalisation, etc., will produce a large number of further modifications of the tone colour.

All these more or less important modifications are designated, by usage, with the name of tone colour, however different their causes seemingly are. An ingenious and successful attempt to base all of them on the aesthetic effect of pitch has recently been made by the well known Berlin teacher of aesthetics and singing, Gustav Engel, who, drawing his conclusion from Helmholtz's opinion that tone colour is due to the sounds being composed of overtones of varying strength, maintains that the preponderance of higher overtones gives the tone sharpness for this reason, because it represents and brings into prominence high pitch along with the low one, that, therefore, all sounds appear as dull and blunt which have no high overtones. In truth, in this way we can explain not only the different qualities of different instruments, such as bassoon and flute, but also those produced by the special kind of bowing, attack, etc. There remains to be considered separately only the undeniable difference of sound according to the different material of which the instrument is made, a difference which probably is to be attributed to the diversity of manner in which the sounds are transmitted to the air. It is known to everybody that the quality of the sounding-board of stringed instruments and the piano is of the utmost importance for the beauty of the tone; it is also well known that it is not the same whether the organ-builder uses tin or lead for his pipes; but it appears that the sides of the pipes, in brass instruments especially the bells, act a similar part as the sounding-boards of stringed instruments; that is to say, they not only give fulness to the sound, but also influence its colour. It is quite possible, however, that even this aspect of the "timbre" may be explained by the strengthening or subduing of high overtones.

Through this identification of tone colour and pitch the importance of the latter grows to an extraordinary extent; it has its effect, first, as absolute pitch of the fundamental tone, which makes the main impression on the ear; secondly, as relative pitch within the range of the particular instrument, where, it appears, the dimensions of the parts that act as sounding-board come into play; thirdly, as characteristic colour of the individual instrument; and, lastly, as specially modulated tone colour in consequence of the peculiar treatment of the instrument.

Thus we see already the possibility of an abundance of different auditory impressions, each of which has a different aesthetic value, that is to say, *touches the soul differently; for every tone sensation becomes a vital experience of our soul.* While, as we have seen, a single tone, sounding with uniform strength and pitch, produces a uniform state of mind, — a mood, — this condition changes from rest to movement, becomes fluctuating, as soon as strength or pitch changes. Both effects are, in the first instance, not *perceived objectively*, but *experienced subjectively*, a fact that should be carefully noted. The longing, "wing expanding" of the horn sound does not present itself to our ears as something outside of us, which we examine as onlookers, but it *directly becomes our own feeling*, *we* long, *we* expand our arms; and similarly we do not see or hear a something ascending and descending, rushing forward and sinking backward, but it is *ourselves* in whom the melody heard lives, *we* are drawn upward and thrust backward, *we* strive and despond, *we* hope and despair. These things are not combinations of ideas suggested by music, not reflections nor associations, they are rather the *essence* of music itself. As a living sentiment it arose in the mind of the composer; into living sentiment, into mental experience, it is transformed directly in the listener. *As soon as music objectivates, it steps out of its most proper sphere of action,* as we shall see later on.

Very beautifully Lotze (loc. cit. p. 79), in reference to a thought of Herder, on the occasion of a criticism of his Calligone, explains how the forms of the visible are transformed into an experience of the soul, on which transformation the elementary effect of the imitative arts is based. As the passage may also serve as a key to the transformation of the forms of the audible into an experience of the soul, I give it in its entirety.

"We, these double beings of body and soul, not only see movements happen, but, also, by our own action produce them. And although we do not directly feel our will in the motion which it imparts to our limbs, still another privilege of our organisation allows here, where the appearance is equal in value to the reality, this kindly delusion. Of the changes which the operating power of our will has produced in the condition of our limbs, from moment to moment a sensation returns to our consciousness; and the changes of this sensation follow with such easy motion every smallest increase or decrease of the tension and relaxation of our muscles, that in this mirrored image of its effects produced, we immediately feel the will at work, and imagine that we accompany it in all the variations of its increase and diminution.

"Thus only we learn to understand movements and to appreciate their significance. Without these recollections any outward movement we observed would only be the incomprehensible fact that formerly something was here and now it is there, and that in the meantime it was in places between the two terminals. Only this own inward experience of action and passion enables us to enjoy the bolder or easier flight of a rising line, and to feel offended by a sudden check of its equal course; only because we feel ourselves the happiness of the equilibrium of our bodies obtained by the exertion of our own activity or by the favour of outward circumstances, and the anxiety of unsteadiness arising from an unfavourable shifting of their parts, — only for this reason equilibrium or want of equilibrium in the distribution of masses are conditions which we observe with the interest of sympathy. And now, after thousands of these little sensations have made us acquainted with the outlines of our bodies and the forms of our limbs, and have explained to us what fullness of elasticity, what delicate excitability and patient strength, what lovely fragility or firmness, slumber in each separate part of these outlines, — now we also are able to understand the strange form.

"And not only do we penetrate into the life-feelings

of that which stands near to us in nature and kind, into the happy flight of the bird, or the graceful agility of the gazelle; not only do we draw together the sensitive fibres of our mind into the smallest possible compass, in order to participate dreaming in the narrowly circumscribed existence of a mollusc, and in the monotonous enjoyment of its opening and shutting its shell; we not only sympathetically expand ourselves into the slender forms of the tree, whose delicate twigs are animated with the pleasure of graceful moving and bending; but, with a presaging power of interpretation that can dispense with any definite remembrance of our own form, we are able to comprehend even the strangest forms of a curve, of a regular polygon, of any symmetrical arrangement of points, as a place of organisation, or as an arena in which to move with nameless powers appears to us as a characteristic happiness in whose enjoyment we are able to participate. And thus *all forms of space* produce an aesthetic effect in us, in so far as they are *symbols* of a peculiar weal or woe that we may *experience ourselves.*"*)

---

*) It was doubtless this disquisition of Lotze's that led Dr. Heinrich Wölfflin in his Dissertation "Prolegomena zu einer Psychologie der Architektur" (Munich, 1886), to the assertion quoted by Dr. Arthur Seidl in his Dissertation "Vom Musikalisch Erhabenen", that the impression made by architecture on our feelings rests solely on the fact that "we involuntarily endeavour to imitate the strange forms with our organisation, in other words, that we judge the feelings of architectural structures according to the bodily condition which they effect in us (p. 13) . . . . Strong pillars arouse in us strong innervations . . . . as if we were ourselves those supporting pillars." Wölfflin also does not omit to make the practical application to music (p. 4): "If we had not the faculty of expressing emotions in tones, we could never understand the significance of foreign tones." I insert these sentences under the text, because I became acquainted with Seidl's pamphlet only after I had delivered my second lecture. We need not quarrel about priority in stating the thought, because Lotze has suggested it clearly enough to all of us. Also the leading thought of the exceedingly attractive publication of Dr. Friedrich von Hausegger, "Musik als Ausdruck" (Vienna 1885), which, unfortunately, in its final conclusions comes to a one-sided glorification of dramatic singing, contains nearly the same idea (Hausegger, however, makes the same mistake as Ed. Grell, supposing that the word, even in the fully developed language, is still an elementary means of expression). With

Although for music the case is essentially different, still it is not difficult to transfer this attractive description, *mutatis mutandis*, to the field of auditory perceptions. The main thing is the *inner experience of the perceived*, so to speak, its *subjectivation*. This transformation of anything perceived into feeling is the more easily done in the case of the audible than in that of the visible, because the audible is not extended in space, but passes in time, and presents itself even in the mere psychological perception as being in constant transition. In reality, indeed, every visual as well as auditory impression is a *nervous* affection. But the former requires time only to obtain a more perfect and more detailed picture, which may be complete in the first moment. The action of hearing on the other hand, consists essentially in connecting auditory impressions following one another, or, to speak more generally, in observing the temporal course of the sounds. The aesthetic enjoyment of musical hearing does not, however, consist in investigating the cause of the sound and of its changes, but in the pleasurable perception of the successive conditions of the soul produced by it, and in fully giving oneself up to the objectless affections aroused by it.

It even appears that, as with visual perceptions, so also in the auditory enjoyment the *remembrance of what we ourselves have experienced*, the *feeling of our own corporeity*, plays a chief part; so that the comparison shows a much closer parallelism than appears at first sight. For we are enabled by nature to produce sounds ourselves, we even habitually manifest the disposition of our soul just as well by tones—namely, in the sound of our language and even in real singing, — as by visible movements of our body, by gestures. For although the man of modern culture only rarely gives free course to his emotions to such extent that the gesture will step out of the conventional track and become real expression, and that the voice will cast away the equally conventional forms of language, and, in cheering and groaning, in cries of jubilation or lamentation, become real music — yet, thank God, we have not lost the understanding of the natural meaning, of the intrinsic significance, of gestures as well

---

Hausegger's book I did not become acquainted until after the conclusion of my lectures.

as of the passionate utterances of the voice. By the latter I mean no more a well ordered melody than by the former a characteristic dance or an artistic pantomime. In both cases I rather refer to the most primary elements, the very simplest motions; in the one to the longing expanding of the arms, the inclining towards anything, or the warding off, the turning away; in the other, to the gladsome outburst or the shrill cry, the joyous shout of welcome or the horrified silence, the dull, voiceless despair. And thus I think it is not a daring thing to assert that also the movements of tone are felt by us sympathetically as perfectly intelligible manifestations of conditions and processes of the soul; that in observing their succession and experiencing them in our own soul, there must be a truly wonderful refinement and specialisation of sentiment, such as we cannot fathom even approximately by mere reflection on our own feeling — in other words, that music not only beats all philosophy, but appears to be destined in an eminent manner to enrich and fructify the life of the soul by compelling souls that feel less intensely or less delicately, to take part in the richer emotions vouchsafed to heaven-favoured artists.

It is not my intention to go more deeply into details by investigating the aesthetic value of certain combinations of tones or rhythmical figures, and, perhaps, by demonstrating which formations exactly correspond to this or that affection. For, in the first place, the question is not about the *expression* of emotions, but, as we shall see and further prove, music moves the soul only in a fashion analogous to that of the emotions, without pretending in any way to awaken them (wherefore it is of no consequence that quite heterogeneous affections have similar forms of movement and can, therefore, be "expressed" by the same music, as Hanslick rightly remarked); but I should also, by such an attempt, act contrary to my expressed intention not to treat of anything technical.

But I have already indicated the general foundation of those relations between movements of tone and movements of the soul, namely, the fact that increasing pitch, strength, and rate of movement, have the significance of positive forms of movement, of coming forward, of a more energetic manifestation of the will, and that the contrary has the meaning of negative development. Why is this so? To this question we hardly need a special answer; for self-observation proves to us that every increase in the energy of our will, every increase of emotion, raises our voice without our knowing it, that with every increase of excitement we speak not only more loudly, but also more quickly, and that, when we become calmer again, the pitch of our voice becomes lower, its strength reduced, its quickness less rapid.

Accordingly it is probably not by chance that we are more forcibly compelled to feel in ourselves, or to subjectivate, those tones that lie within the range of the human voice itself. The feeling that we ourselves can produce the tones heard, undoubtedly is of some importance in this matter. But its influence is not restricted to such an extent that each individual would be moved only by the tones attainable by his own voice. The range of these tones rather extends over the whole compass of the human voice; and a certain power of sympathy which can be more easily divined than expressed in words, and which, without doubt, has its last roots in love, gives the strongest hold upon our soul just to those tones which belong to the range of voice of the other sex. This power decreases, it cannot be denied, the more the tones approach the extreme limits above and below, that is to say, if, generally, the female voice and the instruments akin to it, namely, violin, viola, oboe, and clarionet, attract and move most forcibly the man, and the female soul is affected most vehemently by the male voice, and the horn and cello, that are akin to it, still we have to state that this sympathetic power is less prominent in the high clear soprano and the deep bass, and that also the instruments lose more and more the power of directly exciting sympathy, the more they depart from the centre of the tone region. Violins in high positions and double-basses in their exclusive depth hardly affect the soul directly; we feel with more or less distinctness that their melodies remain *outside of us*, we hear them more *objectively*, than *subjectively*. By this they gain a special importance for those branches of music in which this art is made to appear not merely as subjective, but as objectivating, as *representing*. On this point, however, I shall have more to say in my third lecture.

The strength of the tones also greatly influences our

behaviour towards them. This is not so evident in the direction of the weak, because naturally even the most evanescent *pianissimo* finds an equivalent in our inner life, be it dreamy musing, or tremulous foreboding, or anxious listening, etc. But the thundering power of trombones and tubas, as well as the piercing shrillness and the ringing clang of trumpets, are in too harsh disproportion to the strength of the human voice to affect us sympathetically, — the former as male voices, or, still less, the latter as female voices. These instruments consequently appear in an eminent degree as objective, or, what means the same thing, as dramatic or epic; and the fact that the classical composers, in purely instrumental works, almost completely exclude them from rendering the melody, plainly enough demonstrates that they looked upon their art as a subjective one, while, on the other hand, it is quite natural that the objectivating music which develops more and more in modern times, requires them in ever increasing measure.

The enormous power of the *fortissimo* of the full orchestra with its three trumpets, four horns, three trombones, and possibly several other gigantic bass instruments undoubtedly exerts also an elementary influence on our sensation; but it can hardly be subjectivated as a manifestation of our inner life; it rather stands opposite to us crushing and annihilating as the superior power of *something outside of us*, producing thus the effect of the *sublime*, which we admire in rapture while, at the same time, conscious of our own smallness we are filled with awe by its greatness.*) But as Schiller, towards the close of his

---

*) Also this idea I find in Seidl's book (p. 85): "The sublime will make manifest our inability to put our individual organisation on a par with the immense, by its towering above this individuality.... or better, it will excite its conception in the subject by means of the fact that we fail *to conform ourselves to it.*" He has this thought from Wölfflin's dissertation (p. 12), who continues by saying: "We feel the impossibility of putting ourselves on a par with the immense— our joints are loosened—", a remark that explains the peculiar phenomenon of *giddiness* which the sublime awakens whenever the subject does not succeed in finding in itself the fixed point that is imperishable. Still more distinctly Seidl says p. 82: "The human voice is the measure for the power of all other instruments." For the rest I cannot reconcile myself to Seidl's con-

treatise on the sublime, says so beautifully of imitative art, that it gives only the appearance of the sublime, not its reality, we can, in a similar manner, require the same for music, and expect from the sublime in music just as in the other arts, that it will steel our mind and give fresh strength to our susceptibility of the merely beautiful. He says:

"Sometimes a single sublime emotion is sufficient to give back at once to the fettered spirit its entire elasticity . . . . As long as man was only the slave of physical necessity, as long as he had not found a way out of the narrow circle of his needs, and did not divine the lofty Godlike freedom in his breast, so long the *intangible* in nature could only remind him of the limits of his imagination, and the *destructive* in nature only of his physical impotence. Thus he was compelled to pass by the former (the intangible) with fear and trembling, and to turn away from the latter in horror. But no sooner does free contemplation make room for him in the blind rush of the natural forces, and no sooner does he discover amidst this flood of phenomena something lasting in his own breast, than the wild masses of nature around him begin to speak quite a different language to his heart, and the relatively great outside himself is the mirror in which he beholds the absolutely great within himself. Fearlessly and with pleasure mingled with awe, he, then, approaches those frightful products of his imagination, and intentionally calls up the whole power of this faculty to represent what is infinite for the senses, in order that, failing in this attempt, he may feel all the more vividly the superiority of his ideas over the highest that the senses can achieve."

The superhuman in the form of superhuman strength of tone and of expansion of the range of tone upwards and downwards, contrasted in this way with the human,

---

ception of the sublime, because he tries to draw too much into it (namely, also the stepping beyond the pure line of beauty caused by the preponderance of the elementary over the formal). But I gladly accept his definition: "Sublimity is *infinity suggested by an objective greatness or strength that is overpowering, transcending far beyond human analogy, and leading the mind beyond all proportion appreciable by the senses*," recognising thereby the conditional possibility of subjectivation of the sublime.

cannot, indeed, completely be absorbed by the subject so that it would be intelligible as the utterance of human sentiment. Still it can be experienced humanly, in as far as it can enter our feelings as a phantom, shaking them, in the way explained by Schiller, with the double power of the sublime, at the same time depressing and elevating, destroying and re-animating. Its power, however, will always be conquered in the musical work of art by the purely human re-asserting itself, by the return to degrees of strength and pitch which bring the subjective sentiment again into the foreground and replace the passiveness of the will by its active exercise.

We must not overlook, however, that, by way of gradual heightening, it is quite within the power of the musical artist so to steel, strengthen, and expand the human feeling that it can experience even the *fortissimo tutti* as the expression of the grandeur of the human mind and will, developed to their fullest power. This Beethoven often has succeeded in accomplishing.

But not only does what is too powerful, or too high or too low, refuse subjectivation if presented to us without preparation; we have, rather, to state that a whole category of qualities which have, as common notion, the ugly, are refused by our feelings as "unsympathetic", that is to say, are heard not subjectively, but objectively. Here, too, however, many gradations are possible. Certain instruments, the bassoon, for instance, possess a tone colour which, in the first instance, absolutely repels, and does not touch "sympathetically", but has a comic or ridiculous effect. This quality, of course, is most prominent when they are contrasted with other instruments of a nobler sound, and Haydn, for instance, has oftentimes made capital use of this contrast. But the effect is diminished to a great extent, when such an instrument is used either altogether by itself, as a solo instrument, or in combination with other instruments of a similar quality. It is then as when we become accustomed, on nearer acquaintance, to the repulsive outward appearance of a person, and at last completely cease to be aware of it. This ridiculous quality attaches especially to instruments whose tone we call "nasal",— besides the bassoon, principally to muted trumpets and, in a less degree, to the oboe. It appears that the expression "nasal" is so aptly chosen for this that it even implies the psychological cause for this repulsive effect. Apparently the human singing voice is the standard by which we measure the aesthetic value of the "singing" of instruments; and consequently all instruments whose tone reminds us of any morbid affection of the human voice, must touch us just as disagreeably as the singing of a person suffering from a cold. To no one can such a thing be sympathetic; the place of the inner experience of the sentiment expressed in music, is taken by a sensation of pity, which, of course, may be diametrically opposed to the sentiment of the music. The melancholy effect of certain tone colours must be traced back to this. Both, however, the ridiculous as well as the miserable, are aesthetic values arising from the want of subjectivation. There is no doubt that music, when it wants to objectivate, can make characteristic use of such colours to a great extent and for very different purposes, and we shall have to consider this more in detail later on. At present we have only to state what are the *elementary means* of musical art, abstracting as well from the *form-giving principles* which make music an *art*, as from all associations, which, whether intended or not, add on to the purely musical perceptions others, that either give to the musical perceptions a different value, or, on the contrary, are altered in their aesthetic value by them.

Looking back upon the result of our considerations, we see that the elementary effect of music consists in this: Combinations of tones striking our ears have peculiar aesthetic values according to their properties of pitch and strength, in consequence of our own natural disposition to produce tones ourselves, and to express by our voice the conditions and experiences of our inner life; they are perceived not as being outside of us, but subjectively, that is to say, as being experienced within ourselves while we hear them. We had to state more specially that, in general, rising of pitch, growing of strength, and increase of the pace of this rising and growing, appear as positive development, as increase of energy, vital power, or will; and that, on the contrary, falling of pitch, diminishing of strength, and decrease of the pace of this falling and diminishing, appear as negative development.

The total effects of the various combinations of these factors are, accordingly, movements of the soul corresponding exactly to those movements that are experienced in affections like longing, joy, sadness, anger, fright, fear, etc., but sharply distinguished from them by the fact that they are altogether objectless, severed from all relation to reality, without that "remainder of earthliness" that to bear would be painful. Although all music, and the best in particular, most probably has arisen from a mood of the composer in which the actual world, fortune or misfortune, fulfilled or disappointed hopes, bore a part, it is just the glorious side of art that the work elevates the creator himself, that the plaint which his tortured heart pours forth in sounds, comforts him like soothing balm by the beautiful form it has taken. The relation to the visible world from which his creation emanated, disappears even for the artist himself; his mood becomes generalized by being poured into the forms of the musical work of art; and it is a hyena's work worthy of little gratitude that is carried on with great delight in modern times by our all too industrious aesthetic analysts, when, by consulting sketch-books and diary notes that were by no means intended for publicity and posterity, they follow up the roots of the musical work of art down into the soul of the composer, and are happy on finding at last the clod of earth from which the flower drew its juice of life.

The answer to the question regarding the elementary factors of musical effect has become also the answer to the question regarding the substance of music, that is to say, in the first instance, of absolute music, of music that freely emanates from the heart, and that does not want to be anything else than what, as spontaneous out-pouring of the artist's sentiment, it must be. In what the essence of musical *form* consists, we shall have to consider in our next.

II.
Form-giving Principles:
Harmony and Rhythm.

The movement of the human voice in tonic, dynamic and agogic*) changes, as we have seen, is to be referred to the innate *impulse to impart*. As prompted by this impulse the manifestations of our emotions have a merely natural expression, though one capable of awakening sympathy, that is to say, of causing us to experience personally what we hear, as we explained above. Another impulse, then, namely the *impulse to play*, comes in, giving these manifestations of our emotions a well ordered and pleasing form. Th. Fechner, in his "Vorschule der Aesthetik" (Part 1, page 54), by saying "that man, to find pleasure in the receptive occupation with a subject, must find in it a variety connected in a uniform manner," states as a general principle for all artistic creation, the uniform connection of the manifold. This manifestation of the impulse to play may have for its object either to impart to the communication an intensified interest for him to whom it is addressed, or to give purely subjective pleasure to the subject. The latter is probably that which determines the artist, the former the consequence which naturally follows from this. But the former object may be taken into account by an artist who creates with reflection, not with ideal spontaneity.

Hanslick, in his much read work on "The Beautiful in Music", says that for music there is no prototype in nature. This statement must be admitted in as much as really nothing audible in nature has such a regulated and pleasing course as, for instance, even the simplest folksong. But Hanslick makes a mistake when he feels obliged to assume such a "beautiful object in nature" for the other arts (excepting, strangely enough, architecture). This statement may be maintained, with comparative ease, for painting and sculpture, which, under circumstances at

---

*) This term (from ἀγωγή, the Greek word for "time") has been introduced by Riemann to denote all changes of the *tempo*, especially those that take place in the smallest rhythmical combinations. (*Translator's note.*)

least, can confine themselves to mere imitations of nature. But what about poetry? If Hanslick says that nature knows no sonata, no overture, no rondo; it is equally indisputable that it knows no sonnet, no ode, no rondel. Or is not what distinguishes a sonata from a rondo just as much a mere form as what distinguishes the rondel from the sonnet? But nature knows, according to Hanslick, genre-pictures, idylls, tragedies! There Hanslick overlooks that just what distinguishes the tragedy from a misfortune that has actually happened, is the artistic representation, the beautiful appearance of reality instead of the reality itself which is disturbed by a thousand interfering circumstances.*)

But is such an imitation, such an imaginary representation, really denied to music, is it less within its possibility, than, for instance, within that of painting? Painting, in representing, for instance, a summer's day in the country, can only imitate the visible, and must leave it to the imagination of the looker-on to supply what is wanting — the warm air redolent of luscious aroma, the chirping of the grasshoppers and the jubilations of the birds, etc.; does music remain, to any considerable extent, or even at all, behind painting? Beethoven's *Sinfonia pastorale* might rout many an excellent landscape painter, although here music is not even quite at home, but encroaches on the domain of the sister arts. But why does the painter paint a landscape? Is it in order to portray on canvas in tiny dimensions what stands before him, in grand proportions,

---

*) Neither is the drama benefited by the illusion being carried to such extent that even all kinds of accessories of no necessary connection with the course of the action, are represented in true likeness to nature. Who has not been annoyed by seeing, on the stage, accumulations of dummy personages, such as promenaders, market goers, etc., and this all the more the more lively their behaviour? For, strictly speaking, only those persons ought to find a place in the drama that exert an influence on the main plot. The drama, too, is not a mere imitation on the stage of a piece of real life, but is an artistic representation, an idealisation, a logical concatenation of actions, for the purpose of producing a series of emotions that, in their entirety, will purify and ennoble the soul. The historical painter will also produce a greater effect, not by multiplying the figures, but by eliminating, as far as possible, everything that is not calculated to strengthen the chief idea, that is to say, by idealising.

in nature? If that were so, the doom of painting would have been signed and sealed by the invention of photography. But the painter paints the piece of nature not as it is, but as he sees it, that is to say, he paints a piece of his emotional life, and only where this is the case, can we speak of the *art* of the landscape painter. Just in the same way the musician may proceed, and, indeed, thus does he always proceed. The musician also in every phrase he writes, in every melody, gives a bit of imitation of nature, that is to say, a bit of his emotional life, painted with the material of the musician instead of that of the painter — with tones instead of colours. Only that with the musician the servile imitation of nature plays a still more subordinate part than with the painter. Could not, for instance, the musician imitate a tempest with more fidelity to nature than a painter? The howling of the storm, the roaring of the sea, the rolling of the thunder are directly perceptible to the musician, and even the lightning he can imitate, because our perception readily lets the ear do duty for the eye when light is to be represented by sounds. But how does the musician accomplish his task? Instead of the bare imitation of nature, which would be quite in his power, he gives an idealised imitation, instead of the howling up and down in continuous change of pitch, he gives the graduated progression through the steps of the scale; instead of the whirling noise of thunder and billows, indifferent in tone and of no interest as to rhythm, he gives well regulated harmonies and recognisable measure of time. What is it that makes him do so? And what are the laws that regulate this idealisation?

If we first inquire about the division of time, about measure, we cannot deny that the idea of partitioning off a space of time into comparable sections is suggested to man by nature; the change of day and night, and the recurrence of the seasons, are, on a large scale, what the undulating movements of a twig moved by the wind, or the regular beat of the flying bird's wings, or the hoofbeats of the horse, or the beating of the human heart are on a small scale. Indeed, our real clock is the heart.*)

---

*) M. Steinitzer, "Ueber psychologische Wirkungen musikalischer Formen" (p. 67) says: "The assumption of a medium tempo which is homogeneous to our life-movement (heart-beat), forms the measure for the comprehension of the others" (quoted by Seidl).

The rate of the movements of our heart, the heartbeat, is the metronome by which we measure not only musical movements, but all movements. It has been shown by scientific investigation (Vierordt), by means of the inductive method, through collecting a large number of opinions, that the impression of the quick and the slow in a sequence of tones, or any sequence of sensations, is produced according as the rate of movement diverges, to the one side or the other, from a medium rate which corresponds to about the normal quickness of the pulse.

In this metronome, however, which is inseparable from us as long as we live, we have only a *standard* for judging time values, not a *division* of the time itself. For though the pulse beat is a proof that the functions of our organisation are continuing regularly, on account of this regular continuance itself we do not become conscious of it. But it does fix the aesthetic value of other divisions of time entering our sensation, in as far as it gives to all slower movements the character of the slow, quiet, and in a higher degree that of the retarded or forcibly restrained, and to all quicker movements the character of the quick, excited, even hurrying. It seems to be established that our movements, especially our walking step, stand in relation to the quickness of the pulse; it is hardly by chance that the normal velocity of walking coincides with the normal quickness of the pulse. Thus it is that the ramming of the steam-hammer recurring after long pauses (of the duration of several pulse beats) appears as slow, even very slow, so slow that the equality or inequality of the intervals escapes our judgment unless we have recourse to special means of control (counting between the different beats); on the other hand we get the impression of quickness from the sequence of the beats of three men threshing together, each of whom strikes about once in every second.

From the comparison of audible divisions of time with the pulse beat, therefore, there results for music the idea of the *tempo*, that is to say, of the aesthetic value of the single units of time into which a tone-movement divides itself for the ear, and which correspond approximately to the pulse beat (*units of counting*, *beats*, or *pulses*).

The *necessity* of dividing a melody into small sections, arises, in the first instance, from the impossibility of comprehending anything passing in time otherwise than in small fragments. At least, the conscious comparing of, and the pleasurable application to, the changes of pitch and strength of tone, would hardly be possible, unless, by a perceptible division, occasion were given to look back, at a certain moment of time, to what had passed. This comparison is made possible, in the first instance, by the *gradation of the change of pitch.*

As we have seen above (1.), the essence of melody is properly the continuous, not graduated, change of pitch; that is to say, the peculiar elementary effects of the rising and falling of pitch attach not to the *graduated* progression through the scale, not to the *skip* from one pitch to another, but to the *raising* or *lowering* of the tone, which, for our sensation, translates itself naturally into a striving upwards or sinking backwards. Now we come to investigate why this continuous change is replaced by the graduated one, notwithstanding which, however, as we have seen, the ear hears as though there were continuous change.

Although tones of different pitch are, as we know, of different qualitative value for our feeling, this different quality could hardly be perceived if they proceeded in continuous change from one pitch to another without resting at certain degrees, even though perhaps by some other means (by dynamic accents, for instance) the division of time might suggest a comparison at certain moments. In order, therefore, to facilitate the comparing of the changes in pitch, these changes are graduated, that is to say, we rest at certain degrees of pitch, and from them proceed to others not by *gliding* over, but by quickly *stepping* over. The selection and number of these steps found suitable for this comparison, is by no means arbitrary. Nature rather has indicated definite ways. We know now, and for about two hundred years past, that what is usually called a tone, namely the single sound of a musical instrument or a human voice, is in reality a complexity of tones of different pitch, and that the lowest of them, that which we commonly believe we hear by itself, is only the strongest of them. This phenomenon of the so-called overtones was first discovered by the acoustician Sauveur (1700), who was born deaf, and it forms the starting-point of the epoch-marking theoretical system of the well known composer Jean Philipp Rameau.

But it did not need this discovery to show musicians

the right way for graduating the pitch. From the times of hoary antiquity, musical practice, and, at least since Pythagoras, also musical theory, have recognised the meaning of the simplest tone ratios, the same ratios which the phenomenon of overtones shows as the first elements of the series of overtones, namely the octave, fifth and fourth, from whose combination all the other intervals of the scale were derived. But long before the halting theory was able to fix definitely the tone ratios, the complete scale had been developed, first as pentatonic scale, which knows no semitone (the so-called old Chinese and Gaelic scale), and very early also as heptatonic scale with semitones alternately after two and three tones, and finally, but also several thousand years ago, in China, India and Greece, as transposition of this heptatonic scale in the complete chromatic scale of twelve steps within the octave. Traces of naturalistic melody formation, that is to say, recollections of the continuous change of pitch, for which the graduated change is to be substituted, are to be found in certain small intervals of the scales of oriental nations (the quarter tones of the Indians, the third-tones of the Arabs, the enharmonics of the Greeks), as well as in the *portamento* of our modern singers.

Both on account of our limited time and special programme, we cannot occupy ourselves more particularly with the various scales on which the nations of antiquity and of the middle ages founded their melodies. But we may emphasise this much as established, that theory, indeed, that is to say the attempted philosophical foundation, has exhibited considerable differences at various periods, but not so practice, at least not in what regards the form of the gradation of pitch. There is, accordingly, every reason for the assumption that our present tone system is not, as some think, a thing depending on the condition of taste, not a free creation of the human intellect, but, in its foundation at least, something in accordance with the nature of our minds, something necessary by nature.

The simple relations of tone which the series of harmonics suggests, form the foundation of harmony, in the first instance of the major harmony; as the strict opposite of this appears the minor harmony, which, as it seems, was the more favourite one with the nations of antiquity. The fact of a tone belonging or not belonging to the harmony taken as starting point, constitutes the ideas of consonance and dissonance, which attain their full significance only when several parts moving simultaneously emphasise the question of compatibility more sharply than is the case with tones following each other in melodic succession.

The idea of key, or, as it is now called, of tonality, simply results from the natural indolence of the perceiving mind, or, as Lotze more euphemistically expresses it, from the economy of perception, which tries to hold fast what it has, and, therefore, understands the second thing not as another separate entity, but as something that receives its peculiar value from its relation to the first.

Thus the scale results as a scheme for melodic motion dependant on harmonic relations. Lotze says (page 468): "For our modern feeling the charm of a melody never consists in the mere motion through different pitch, but always in this, — that this motion, however incalculable in other respects its swing and direction may be, still at certain moments is sure to touch certain definite steps of the scale which stand to each other in harmonic relations, well-known and always present to our memory. Melody does not soar up and down, like a bird, in the empty realms of the air, but it moves, as we say, on a "ladder", the scale; our enjoyment of it consists in the certain anticipation that its next step will not sink into indefinite space, but that it will reach one of the steps which, in the general organisation of the realm of sound, have been fixed, not only for this melody, but also for every other. This is not a special peculiarity of musical beauty, but a general quality of beauty of every kind ... In no free game, not even in the throwing of balls, could an interest be conceived, were it not that the quite arbitrary motions which we produce are only the introduction to the manifestation of a series of effects connected by natural laws. It is not the unrestrained freedom by itself that delights us, but the simultaneous perception of a necessity which is constantly ready not only to limit the licence of that freedom, but also to impart to it support, aid, and security. For this reason music, too, delights in the free swing of melody through different tones, merely because this freedom affords it an opportunity of becoming conscious of the firmness and the reciprocal relations of those points of rest between which this free motion takes place."

It may be doubted whether music as it presents itself now when the rate of movement in time and the change of pitch in the region of tone that has become measurable by the scale, have been determined — is really still the same as we felt bound to define it when explaining the elementary factors. Has it not, by these relations of the tones, received an altogether new complexion? Do not the elementary factors appear as subordinate and unimportant if compared with harmony and metre?

It can in no wise be denied that, to a certain extent, for the consideration of the essence of music the danger exists of falling into formalism and of overlooking, in following out the manifold relations of pitch and duration of tone, the chief thing; namely that the melody movement must be, first and above all, the free out-pouring of emotion. On the other hand, indeed, the *form* of music determined by harmony and metre, is indispensable; in fact it is through it that the art becomes art.

I have already (1.) pointed out that music, by the irresistible elementary effects of melodic, dynamic and agogic changes forces even the poorer-souled man to participate in the richer spiritual life of genius. Let us now realise more accurately what this means. If we call to mind any of the magnificent long-drawn Adagios of Beethoven, we find therein such a variety, such a multiplicity of shades of sentiment, such a wealth of manifold niceties of expression, that really the sympathetic listening to such a movement can be compared to the hearing and seeing of a drama, which likewise leads the soul through a series of emotions, logically connected, elevating and purifying.

A great part-of the magic sway such a work of art exerts upon the listener, depends on the beautiful form in which the vigorous and healthy feelings sympathetically accost us; this beautiful form does not produce its effects upon all persons in the same decisive manner; for it requires *comprehension* and loving *application, full attention.*

The *"illimitable cultivability of the ear"*, as Wagner calls it, is the faculty that increases with practice, of apprehending tone relations. People that occupy them selves little or not at all with music, find pleasure only in the *simplest* harmonic and melodic turns, in the simplest, clearest thematic arrangements, in the simplest, directly intelligible rhythmical combinations; and the works of a Bach, a Schumann, a Wagner, a Brahms, are to them, to use their own expression, *too learned*, that is to say, too complicated. This is more than a mere phrase, and all the arguments in the world will not persuade these amateurs into a liking for the above-named composers. I emphatically repeat that practice and goodwill are required for the understanding of a great complicated musical work of art. If the whole is not to fall asunder in a number of loosely connected separate impressions, each of which is of little intensity, — if, rather, each is to support, raise, heighten the others either by analogy or by contrast, then not only the comprehension of the separate is required, but also conscious attention to the connection, which means a strong exertion of the memory and synthetic activity of the mind. In other words, when the higher forms of art begin, the possibility ceases of getting on with mere passive reception of the impressions, be it ever so willing and devoted, and the necessity for active co-operation arises.

Not that *special technical knowledge* is indispensable for the enjoyment of musical works of art of the highest order; such knowledge is no more required for the enjoyment of the beauty of Beethoven's Ninth Symphony, than for that of the beauty of Cologne Cathedral. But what is certainly indispensable, is practice and preparation by the hearing of simpler music. We can easily convince ourselves of this when we observe how people who themselves do not practise music at all, and perhaps do not even know the notes, but who hear a great deal, are capable of giving a sound judgment on new works. The professional musician only has names and notions of the details of the technical construction. In these, however, the essence of the work of art is not contained, and by the non-musician who is trained only by listening, they are considered, not as elements of the form, but only in their relation to the substance of the whole.

But the beholder of Cologne Cathedral who is not himself an architect, is at a considerable advantage in comparison with the hearer of the Ninth Symphony who is not a musician. The former quietly stands before the

Cathedral and allows its figure to work on his imagination as long as he chooses; he first understands the construction as a whole and by degrees enters into details; he first comprehends the symmetries of the great outlines, and from these gradually proceeds to appreciate those of the smaller parts. It is otherwise with the hearer of music. Speedily the tone picture passes by his ear, and if he does not succeed in apprehending it at once, the possibility of understanding it better by comparison with what follows, is lost. Everything depends on the sharp comprehension of the smallest formations and their tone relations, that is to say, on the understanding of the most minute symmetries.

In the face of such difficult tasks we can well understand the indispensibility of the double division mentioned already, that of the time into equal sections of a size we can easily grasp, and that of the change of pitch into few steps whose distances are made intelligible to us by the harmonic relations manifested in the nature of sounds.

Listening to music, therefore, like looking at an architectural work of art, is, in its formal aspect, an apprehension of symmetrical formations. But in architecture these symmetrical formations stand side by side at the same time, so that we may, indeed, call the one the counterpart of the other, but also may at any time reverse the order. In music, on the other hand, really always the one thing is first, and the other, the *subsequent, entering into symmetry* with the former, establishing the symmetry, completing it, and, therefore, in a certain sense forming a conclusion. All these corresponding parts, therefore, possess a *concluding force* that more or less makes itself felt, and, in contradistinction to those that have not this concluding force, are called *strong* or *accented*. As the smallest symmetry in music the juxtaposition of two units of counting must appear, of which the second is felt as contrasting with the first; I cannot omit mentioning here that such concluding time.values are made more easily intelligible as such by a slight prolongation, a lingering on them. This lingering, if prolonged to the doubling of the concluding time-value, has as its result the prototype of triple time. As in the smallest symmetry, namely the bar, or measure, we distinguish one strong and one or more weak pulses, so, in a higher order, we distinguish strong and weak measures; that is to say, the measures that form the corresponding part of a symmetry, possess a concluding force, which is the stronger according as the formation concluded by them is larger. Here we must well observe that the original formation cannot consist in the sequence strong-weak, but that the sequence weak-strong must form the starting point. I mention this because the reform of the theory of rhythm which I advocate, starts from this proposition, and combats a contrary mode of conception that of late has taken deep root. This so-called "system of phrasing" keeps many a pen busy at present, and probably will cause many a literary combat in future. My so-called "phrasing editions" of the sonatas of Mozart and Beethoven, of the sonatinas of Clementi and Haessler, as well as of some piano compositions of Bach and Schubert,[*]) try to enforce this consistent conception of thematic formations in the sense of proclitic rhythm (in the order weak-strong), by means of a more complete method of marking. I request those who take an interest in questions of this kind and have not yet had an opportunity of seeing one of my editions, to pay some attention to them when an occasion turns up. In a series of theoretical books, especially in my "Musikalische Dynamik und Agogik", I have fully explained the foundation of this system; my teaching, too, consistently keeps to the points of view indicated.

The symmetrical formations alluded to are the foundation on which the themes of a piece of music are constructed; but between themes that are to form a significant contrast, as a rule, smaller parts are introduced which are wanting in this clearly transparent, crystalline formation. This metrical distinction of larger separate parts of the work of art is supported by analogous harmonic formations. The first form in which the idealising substitution of graduated change of pitch for the continuous change makes the harmonic relations of the tones intelligible, is the adherence to a definite key, that is to say, the restriction to tones that are easily intelligible in their relation to one principal tone, the tonic. The second is the abandoning of his key in favour of one nearly related to it,

---

[*]) Meanwhile other works have been included in these editions so that now they comprise nearly all the standard works of the whole classical piano literature (Translator's note).

and the subsequent return from this strange key to the original one. This appearance of a new key (the modulation) is generally associated with the construction of a new theme, thus helping to distinguish the antithetical parts and to secure greater effects of contrast.

We have not, as yet, devoted a word to the consideration of what, in a narrower sense, is called *Rhythm*, that is to say, of the formations produced by contraction and division, as well as by deviating combinations of contraction and subdivision, of the units of counting. Rhythm, too, must be considered as being originally quite free and not measured. We have pointed out already (1.) that the velocity of the change of strength and pitch of tone produces an elementary effect. By this we meant primarily the difference it makes for our feeling, whether, for instance, the howling storm changes its pitch of tone quickly or slowly. Now we see that, after the substitution of the graduated change of pitch for the continuous change, that change in the rapidity of motion must be transformed into a sequence of tones of different length and of equal or different pitch. Naturally, then, this sequence leads us to compare these different values of duration and thus becomes a direct occasion of an arrangement in equal units of counting. As a matter of fact rhythm is older than the plain measure, that is to say, the oldest melodies did not move in equal and unvaried units of time, but in simple rhythms repeated regularly, as has been proved alike in the case of ancient Greek music, and in that of the western music of the Middle Ages.

If we consider the immense wealth of graduated relations which tones of different pitch, strength, and duration can enter into, the most interesting of which, namely Polyphony, that is to say, the simultaneous sounding of different independent parts, we have not even mentioned — we cannot, certainly, be surprised that the formal may engage the whole interest, nay the entire strength, the entire learning, of a man to such an extent that over it he may forget everything else. The Genius, the artist by vocation, is forced by enthusiasm to give expression to what is going on within him, and the form is to him only the inevitable means of communication. But he who lacks this divine fire will cling to the external which he observes in the works of the inspired Masters, he will imitate their harmonies, their rhythms, their modulations, their thematic constructions. Still, though everyone will admit that everything has been faultlessly and cleverly done, that the form is irreproachable and imposing, never can the fact be obscured that the main thing is wanting, namely, the elementary, the spontaneous outpouring of emotion, for which beautiful melody is only the chosen form, never the end and aim.

We do not mean, however, to say that harmony and rhythm are *only* form, only beautiful appearance, and have no connection with the substance of the work of art. Harmony is a manifestation of the relations of tones given by nature, that is to say, a manifestation of a law that, as everywhere, so here, governs nature in the smallest as in the greatest things, it is a cosmos in itself whose wonders unfold themselves to the astonished gaze in the more radiant form, the more deeply the beholder enters into its contemplation. This law, which may be defined as unity in variety, can be recognized as well in the single melody, — in monody —, as in the combination of several parts, — in polyphony. The composition in full harmonies only represents in a clearer and more obvious fashion the principles of harmony, which equally hold for composition in one part. If the principles of harmony (with the exception of the primary beginnings of the doctrine of consonance and dissonance alluded to above) did not receive any considerable attention until music was written in different parts, this only goes to prove that free, natural invention could deal with the one-part melody without the help of "theory", but that the more complicated apparatus of writing several parts simultaneously, rendered the technique so much more difficult that unschooled naturalness was bound to fail.

If, looking at the polyphony of an orchestral composition, we remember our definition of the significance of the elementary factors, one point forces itself upon our attention with irresistible power, namely this, that in many instances hardly the whole of a polyphonic movement can be subjectivated; but that — as, in listening to a drama, we identify ourselves with one or a few persons who touch us sympathetically, and conceive the others objectively in their relation to us or to those with whom we identify ourselves — so also in the instrumental work only a few prominent parts moving us sympathetically are the real representatives of the subject-matter with which we identify ourselves, while others either appear as remaining outside of us, fighting against us, receding from us, or like delicate tendrils surround us. Naturally, as a rule, the melody proper, which is characteristic of all modern works of art, will be the part that enlists our sympathy.

With regard to the different aesthetic values of high and low tones we have further to remark that in full-voiced compositions the special effect of the different pitch must lose somewhat on account of the various degrees of pitch being represented in a significant manner simultaneously, and this all the more, of course, the less the single voices get an opportunity of free display, of soaring aloft into higher or descending into darker regions of tone. Naturally, therefore, a certain heaviness and monotony will be peculiar to the full-voiced composition as compared with the freely moving monody. On the other hand the simultaneous production of the various colours of different pitch is a new factor of a specific *elementary effect;* even abstracting from the peculiar fact that the tones of different pitch sounding simultaneously either blend together in consonant harmony so as to produce the effect of one compound tone, or that this harmony is disturbed by dissonant elements — the various combinations of high and low tones manifest a quite peculiar, soul-moving quality, as, for instance, the combinations of male voices alone, or of female voices alone, or of male and female voices, or further those of low male voices and high female voices, etc., and similarly with instruments.

As a general rule composers keep the parts of a harmonic passage pretty close to each other, so that the combined compass of the voices occupies either a middle, or low or high position, and accordingly produces its aesthetic effect, and also remains free, by change of this position, to produce effects analogous to those of a single voice rising or falling. But when the parts, instead of rising or falling together in parallel motion, adopt contrary motion, that is to say either depart from each other or draw closer together, then that new effect is produced which opens up, to the musical development, a *third dimension.* While rising and falling appeared to us as a vertical motion, *crescendo* and *diminuendo* as advancing and retiring, that is to say as in a horizontal line running straight forward, we may consider the effects produced by the enlarging and diminution of the distances between the parts as a broadening and narrowing, therefore as being in the direction of a transverse horizontal line. Thus we might say with truth that only in polyphony music has attained its full corporality, its third dimension. —

In order fully to understand the essence of *Rhythm*, we must revert once more to its natural foundation. Our bodily organism carries on its functions in a manner clearly divided into small sections of time, first in the pulsations of the heart, secondly in the breathing; in addition to these two we might mention the shutting of the eyelids repeated at short intervals in order continually to renew the sensitiveness of the retina, from which has arisen the idea of the "twinkling of an eye" — a moment. All these three are by no means unchangeable, nor are they exactly in direct connection with each other. Still it is certain that sudden, violent excitement quickens the beating of the heart, as, on the contrary, terror can cause it to stop; also that the breath of an excited person goes quicker, or, as the saying is, flies; while, on the other hand, quiet respiration, inhaling and exhaling long breaths, is a sign of a quiet mind. Respiration takes place far more slowly than the beating of the heart; on an average six to eight beats of the pulse correspond to a long breath (inhaling and exhaling). While, therefore, we compared the pulse beat with the units of the musical division of time, the so-called units of counting, we shall not be doing wrong by finding an analogy for the respiration in the phrase, as Dr. Fuchs has done in his works on phrasing. If we keep in mind that singing is the natural foundation of music, the eminent practical significance of the phenomenon of breathing for the musical structure becomes manifest. As we can sing only while exhaling, the possible duration of a series of tones that can be rendered in a strictly connected way is approximately determined by the possible duration of exhaling. Consequently every song melody, and, in imitation of it, every other melody, divides itself into a number of small sections which may be compared to breaths. But as the breath itself may be longer or shorter, so the melody divides itself now into longer, now into shorter phrases. The short-windedness or breathlessness of the hurrying sequence of short motives of some scherzo-like movements, as well as on the other hand the long-windedness of Beethoven's melodies, especially in his slow movements, are so familiar to all that I may quote them in order to show that we are not dealing here with idle comparisons, with barren analogies.

The architectural construction of themes referred to above, which renders the comprehension of great forms possible to the apprehending mind by establishing small symmetries that combine in a higher order into greater symmetries, begins, as a rule, with phrases which we must call short or short-winded, but then takes a wider range, and finally not unfrequently exceeds the limits of the human breath to a considerable extent. Such formations, however, do not lose thereby their close relation to human nature, but rather, as it were, enlarge its strength and size, extend and widen out our feelings to the all-embracing, as Schiller's sublime words express it, "Be encompassed, O ye millions!" — — —

If we compare pulse and breathing, we find the former not nearly so variable as the latter. We cannot, therefore, measure so well the rate of the pulse by the rate of respiration, as, on the contrary, the rate of respiration by the rate of the pulse. Naturally, then, the foundation for the musical measurement of time is formed not by the phrasing, but by the "measure", that is to say, by the counting of the units of time proper, that approximately correspond to the pulse beats, and of the small symmetries that first arise from their combinations. The possible deviations from the medium rate of movement do not extend, on the one side, to one half, and, on the other side, to the double of the normal rate of about 75—80 per minute, which appears neither slow nor quick. A rate of 50 pulses per minute appears already as very slow, and a rate of 140 per minute already as very quick. The varying quickness of the *units of counting* very materially determines the *Ethos*, the character of a piece; as *tempo* it forms, as is well known, one of its main marks. The tempo is the substitute for the elementary factor of the velocity of change of pitch and strength of tone, while rhythm only appears as one means of the distinct representation of this change, the other being the gradation of pitch.

It would lead us too far and, in the end, would prove a vain attempt if we were to weigh more particularly all the various combinations of factors which here appear possible. Let it suffice to call to mind that musical theory is a very wide subject whose separate branches: harmony, melody, rhythm, form, can fill large volumes and have filled many. Only in general we may state that harmony and metre awaken a new intellectual interest for this reason, that what in its mere tonic, dynamic, and agogic movement would be but a *natural occurrence*, is transformed by them into an agreeable event that *gives aesthetic pleasure* to the contemplating soul. The measurableness of the values of duration, the recognisable preservation of a unity in the relations of pitch, the easily observable recurrence of equal or similar formations (the melodic-rhythmic motives and phrases) are followed by the perceiving spirit with pleasure. This enjoyment in the order of art, in the cosmic development, associates itself, indeed, as a new factor with the emotion that music produces by means of the elementary factors of pitch, strength, and rate of movement. Its effect is that of ennobling and softening; the natural impulse loses its rude violence, the last remains of dross adhering to music from the earthly passion that gave birth to it, are purged away, and thus the work of art becomes capable of fulfilling what we had already to name as its highest task, namely the ennobling and purifying of the sentiment not only of the listener, but also of the master himself who produced it.

If, before passing to the consideration of what music can effect by means of all kinds of associations of ideas, we survey once more the means of effect of absolute music, that does not intend to be anything but expression of sentiment, that does not want explanations, prefaces or footnotes, and that is without connection with other arts, we have to distinguish the following:

1. The aesthetic effect of pitch, and this in a twofold manner, (a) as actual *change* of pitch, as rising and falling, up and down, and (b) as *fixed different* pitch, as high and low, above and below. The elementary power of change of pitch was not lost when we substituted the graduated transition for the continuous one; our perception, rather, notwithstanding the gradation, which appeared only as a means for the easier recognition of the actual change, held fast

to the continuous transition, in whose sense it understood the graduated one. But on the other hand, instead of possible loss of rude natural efficacy, we gained a great amount of aesthetic enjoyment in the manifold natural relations of tones, which we were able to reduce essentially to two principles opposite to each other like poles, namely the major and minor harmony, the former rising brightly and vigorously, the latter pointing downwards mournfully and gravely. Through these means of easily comparing the degrees of rising and falling we attained the possibility of the construction of larger forms, that is the possibility of greater climaxes and contrasts. We point out once more that in place of simple rising of pitch we have first the rising within the same harmony, next the transition from one harmony to another which appears as heightening, and finally the transition from one key to another heightened one. For the continuous change of pitch, therefore, is substituted, besides the melodic progression, progression of harmony and modulation. The guide through this apparent labyrinth of possibilities of relations of tones, is

Unity in Variety.

the highest law in all artistic creation generally.

The simultaneous sounding of several parts of different pitch we had to designate as a kind of third dimension in music, producing, however, not entirely new effects, but only varied combinations and gradations of those already considered.

2. A second specific means of effect of absolute music is different strength of tone, (a) as *continuous change*, as *crescendo* and *diminuendo*, and (b) as *contrast*, as *forte* and *piano*, etc.

In consequence of the division of time into small sections, which is necessary to make a development of longer duration and a grander plan comprehensible, an increasing and decreasing of strength in large outlines must be replaced by changes in smaller periods or by contrasting dynamic effects. If we assume that stronger emotion will select, as its natural expression, rising pitch as well as increasing strength, every small period of emotion will represent itself, primarily, as a rising and subsequent falling of pitch, and increasing and subsequent decreasing of strength. But in the division of time referred to, there is an essential difference between what regards pitch and what regards strength. The variation of *pitch* can begin again at the point where it was left, and develop further, because this can easily be understood. *Strength*, on the other hand, will not allow such resuming of the degree at which the preceding period ended, but it will have rather to start anew from the zero point, or, at least, from a certain minimum. In other words, each small tone figure will represent in dynamic rather than in tonic aspect, a growing and subsequent vanishing away; it will, as regards strength, develop, in a positive direction, to a certain culminating point, and then take a retrograde course. This period of dynamic development will place certain moments of time in which it culminates, into prominence and suggest to the perception to take these as guiding points for the combination of several units of counting to groups representing a higher unit.

3. The third elementary means of effect of absolute music is the *quickness of change* of pitch or strength. If we consider, instead of the rude formations of nature, the simpler forms of art, that is to say the small independent sections characterized by their tonic and dynamic development, the motives and phrases which the perceiving mind compares to each other, it is clear that the quickness of actual change cannot be observed so easily in different tone figures following each other, as within each one of them. Naturally here again the positive development, namely the increase of velocity will combine most readily with the *crescendo* and the positive melodic development. The means of measuring the increase and decrease of quickness of motion, is the consistent division of time into equal units of counting, whose duration, as we saw, approximately corresponds to the medium velocity of the pulse. We have to distinguish, therefore, (a) the general rate of movement: the *tempo*, which derives its aesthetic value from its relation to the normal quickness of the pulse; (b) the small modifications of the values of counting, on which the elementary effect of *stringendo* and *ritardando* depends: the *Tempo rubato, Mouvement passionel*; (c) a varied form of movement within conditions fixed by the general movement of the units of counting: the *Rhythm*.

Concerning the effect of rhythmical formations, which

we have touched as yet only cursorily, we have to make the supplementary remark that it is to be referred altogether to their relation to the value of the units of counting. The motion in plain units of counting is rhythmically indifferent, it produces its effect merely by the melodic, dynamic and agogic changes. The simplest rhythmical formations properly so called are the *contraction* of several units of counting to one long note, and the *subdivision* of the unit of counting into two or more shorter ones; more complicated formations arise from abnormal subdivision of contracted values (triolets, etc.) and from abnormal contraction of subdivided units (syncopation). In general we have to say about the aesthetic value of these rhythmical means that the contraction of several units of counting appears as a stopping of the motion, and has a retarding, separating, concluding effect; while subdivision gives a fresh opportunity for recognising the continuation of movement, and, therefore, has a stirring, enlivening effect, appears a new beginning.

But the most characteristic effects on our feelings result from the combinations of contraction and subdivision. Amongst them we will mention specially the syncopation, that anxious and exciting formation whose essence consists in this, that at the moments of time when we expect an entry of tone, that is to say at the commencement of the units of counting, none occurs, but the entry does take place between, when we expect none. Syncopation, therefore, combines the retarding of the contraction with the stirring of the subdivision. Finally, we have to take into consideration the *rest*, the interruption of the sounding, which, of course, only as contrast can attain musical significance. It would lead us too much into the detail of technology, were we to discuss in particular the various meanings rests can have. I must confine myself to remarking that rests are not *zero* values, but *minus* values, and that the absence of sound can be felt with a very varying intensity according as the rest takes the place of a more or less important value. While rests following tones that form a natural conclusion have scarcely any importance for our feelings, others that interrupt a phrase, and particularly those that occur before the centre of gravity, have a frightening, alarming, breath-stopping effect.

The eminent significance of rhythm as means of expression of the *subjective sentiment* is manifest enough. Still we cannot reckon it under the elementary factors, because it pre-supposes the gradation of pitch and the division of time into equal parts; its relation to agogic effects, to the acceleration and retardation of the movement, is clear; both have a common root; but rhythm is an artistic formation belonging to the same category as melodic formation within the regulated sequence of the scale. This can easily be seen from the fact that its essential effect is fully attained only when it is continued according to the general rules of art, that is to say, when it is repeated or contrasted. Elementary effects, generally speaking, are only those that result without active co-operation of the mind; but the mind has actually begun its operations when it compares durations of time or recognises relation of pitch. Once again I must refer to the howling storm in order to explain what are the elementary effects of changes of pitch, strength, and quickness; but let it not be forgotten that these elementary effects remain when art substitutes graduated changes for the continuous changes, and thus gives the intellect an incitement to exert its activity in following the movements that have become measurable.

Quite another kind of activity, however, is demanded of the mind, when music ceases to be subjective, when it undertakes to describe, to paint; for while the observation of the formal construction, the control of harmonic and rhythmic relations, is, after all, only a perception of something present, an acceptation of something offered, objectivating music requires that the listener should add something, that his imagination should work *productively*. Of this we shall have to speak in our next.

III.

Associative Factors:

Characteristic Expression, Tone-painting, Programme Music.

In the investigation of the elementary factors of the musical impression as well as of the form-giving principles, we repeatedly had occasion to observe that music has

the faculty of objectivating; for we recognised that certain
quantitative or qualitative sound phenomena that are either
too alien from human nature or affect it, instead of sympathetically, in an antipathetic or even pathological manner,
more or less opposed themselves to subjectivation; that
which is too low, like that which is too high, did not
appear as adapted for the expression of subjective sentiment; likewise that which is too powerful in the strength
of tone could not be absorbed by the subject, but rather
entered our sensation as a phantom with the effect of
the sublime. We now set about seeking intentionally all
that music can do as an objectivating art; we will throw
some light on the associative factors by means of which
music can produce in our imagination the representation
of definite persons, situations, and, in general, events of
the outward world, which have a connection with music
only in so far as the sensations produced by them are
similar to those that the applied forms of movement of
music are known by experience to produce. Already we
can see that all objectivating music is reflected, that is to
say, not direct expression of sentiment, but expression of
sentiments engendered by imagining oneself in a certain
situation, therefore expression of imagined sentiments of
others. In other words, we have to recognise that the
notions subjective and objective are to be taken in a
sense almost contrary to the general acceptation; for we
find that those composers who treat music as an imitative,
objectivating art, are usually considered as the more subjective ones, as those with whom subjectivity is more
prevalent, while to the classics, with whom, as we have
seen, the art remains quite subjective, objectivity is generally attributed. Apparently two ideas are here confounded
that have nothing in common, or a word is used for two
altogether different things. Finally, however, it appears
that music when it undertakes to objectivate, is forced to
let recede into the background the only thing that in
purely subjective, absolute music might be called objective, in as far as it occupies the mind with its contemplation, namely the formal of the harmonic and metric
structure and the development of rhythms (therefore the
symmetrical, the architectonic), while it utilises to a higher
degree the elementary factors, that is to say, those that
most directly effect subjectivation (melodic, dynamic, and

agogic elements). Consequently, objectivating music usually (more exactly: as far as its individual form is concerned) will be a less perfect object of *Art*; the specific beauty of music which consists just in the perfect architecture of harmony, rhythm, and metre, will appear in a less degree, because the intentional reference to the actual world, the intention of characterizing, necessarily must bring forward that disparity of proportion and those manifold deviations from the ideal lines of beauty in which all individuality consists. But let us not begin at the end, but rather proceed successively from the modest appearance of associative factors in absolute music, to the radical objectivation of the most extreme programme musicians.

It is by association that horn fanfares remind us of forest and hunting, trumpet blasts of fight and victory, or, at least, of warlike spirit and festive pomp, that the sound of oboes and bassoons calls up before our imagination rural scenery with herd and flock. For we know the horn as signal horn of the hunters (though now chiefly confined to the stage); the cavalry trumpet and the shepherd's pipe are familiar enough to us as a sort of natural music, which art imitates; for nobody will object that because the pipe is made by man it is, therefore, a product of art — as, for the painter, houses are part of a landscape, so are hunting-horn and shepherd's pipe for the musician. Still, the fact that the cuirassier does not give the signal for charge on an oboe, and that the shepherd in his quiet, peaceable occupation in snug solitude does not love the blast of trumpets, has a deeper reason too. For the excitement of battle, as, in a less degree, also of the hunt, requires greater strength of tone, and even the harmonic rigidity caused by the limitation to the component parts of a single harmony with, at the most, incidental touching of foreign tones, is more suited for the situation than the chromatic multisonance and harmonic mobility of the wood wind instruments. The importance of their being heard at a distance also necessitates for the trumpet and the horn the use of *longer* tones, while it is more natural to the shepherd to imitate on his instrument the light mobility of the birds' voices. In passing we may remark that the Alpine herd, whose attention is directed by nature to the grand, prefers an instrument of the horn species to the pipe.

In a similar way the religious solemnity which we

associate with the sound of trombones, is not only the result of our experience that trombones are used by preference for the accompaniment of slow Chorale singing; unquestionably, rather, the sound of this instrument appears to our sensation as a gradation of the human voice towards the grand, the majestic, without any screaming; according to what we have seen above, therefore, it is adapted either to widen our feeling into the great, the broad, that is to say, to elevate us, or, on the other hand, to stand opposite us with the effect of the sublime: in both cases it appears as the appropriate organ for the solemn devotion of divine service. As far as we can determine now, with the Greeks, too, the solemn religious songs (the Spondees) had the same slow emphatic movement as our hymns, and even the Hebrews, and still earlier the old Egyptians, used in their Temple service instruments of the trombone kind with a strong, far-reaching tone.

We have seen already that a different aesthetic value attaches to the instruments according to their relation to the human voice; but perhaps also the similarity to certain animals' voices peculiar to instruments whose sound is far removed from that of the human voice, gives them a special characteristic meaning. The similarity of the higher wood wind instruments, especially of oboes and flutes, to birds' voices is obvious; for the explanation of their rural character, therefore, this circumstance must not be lost sight of. The gruff voice of the bassoon, especially in its lowest tones, and still more of the now obsolete ophicleide or the modern bass tuba, makes us imagine involuntarily some uncouth animals, be they roaring bulls or lions, or even fabulous monsters like the dragon that Siegfried slays. Why does it appear to us now almost ridiculous that in the year 585 B. C. the flute-player Sakadas got a prize at the Pythian games with a *nomos* that represented in tones the combat of Apollo with the dragon Python? Why does it appear to us as ridiculous? Only for this reason, that the weakly and pretty high sounding voice of the flute appears as too tiny to paint in tones a monster like Python.

Thus we have already advanced so far as to recognise the direct parallelism of pitch and the dimensions of beings whose voice the tones are to represent; this parallelism probably has to be referred to the fact already mentioned, that the vibrating mass is larger with low tones than with high ones.

The high region of tone appears to us as light, bright, mobile, winged, ethereal; the lively vibrations of higher tones not only carry us upwards, but also, when we do not subjectivate them, appear as *an above;* the heavy, slow vibrations of the low tones not only draw us downwards, but also can represent *a below*; the low region of tone is the dark, horrific, gloomy, spectral. The powers of darkness sing bass, the angels of light, soprano.

These various observations show, in the first instance, a significant meaning of pitch and of the timbre related to it. That is to say, when the musician, instead of simply pouring out his emotion in tones, undertakes to represent events of the world of phenomena or mental conditions of others, even the selection of timbre and of degree of pitch affords him many very important means of characterising. Let us think, for instance, of the dark colour of Brahms' Rhapsody, which as well by the selection of an Alto voice for the solo (and, later on, the selection of the accompanying male choir kept in quite sombre tints), as by the low position of the accompanying instruments, at once transports us not only into the heart of the queer misanthrope himself, but also into the landscape in keeping with his state of mind, into the density of the forest into which only here and there a glaring ray of light falls when he bends the twigs asunder. Or let us think of the Lohengrin prelude with its four solo violins in highest pitch without any other support, do they not appear as a something floating in the loftiest sunlit heights, gradually sinking down to the earth, as Wagner really intended to represent by it the carrying down of the holy Grail by the angels? Or let us think of the striking effect produced by the sound of the muted stringed instruments in the tenor aria before the thunder-storm in Haydn's "Seasons"; do we not see there, as it were, the glowing air that cannot be breathed and that paralyses all the senses by its sultriness? Or, to take an example where not only sensations of vision or touch, but even of smelling are awakened by music — think of the beginning of the evening scene before Hans Sachs' workshop in the second act of the "Meistersinger" where to the words "How breathes the lilac so mild, so strong and full" the swelling, welling sound of the horns *(pianissimo)* over the gently floating *tremolo* of the stringed instruments, conjures up before our imaginations, almost in transporting delusion of our senses, the fragrance of the midsummer night!

As *pitch* of tone, so also *strength* of tone gives rise to associations, if once we have been directed to hear objectively. As the low, so also the weak is the dark; as the high, so also the strong is the bright; night-pieces, therefore, do not admit a real *forte*, and the breaking in of light demands *crescendo* or sudden *forte*, as Haydn, in his "Creation", to the words "Let there be light" has given a model for all time The veiled light of the moon cannot well, indeed, dowithout high pitch, but it requires mutes, or, at least, *piano* and *pianissimo*. If strong low tones can appear to us now as powerful and gigantic, now as uncouth and churlish, on the other hand staccato runs of low bass tones in *pianissimo* have certainly nothing heavy about them, but they can rival the highest flute and violin figures in shadowy fleetness and spectral immateriality.

We have to distinguish three degrees of the characteristic meaning of muical elements. The first consists in this, that generally a piece of music is suited to a particular object. The second, which requires more attention to details, conssts in this, that, in the connection of music with the word or mimic representation, or both, the musical effect is in keeping with that of the other arts. And finally, that which requires the greatest precision of expression, when music undertakes to represent without the aid of word or gesture an action, or any piece of real life, indicated by a title, a programme, a poem previously known, or by some similar means. We see that these three degrees moreand more recede from the fundamental essence of music This does not mean, however, that the artistic effect must be of less and less value; for we must not forget that music, from its connection with other arts, and even from the mere awakening of associations of ideas, derives a more or less important enhancement of its effects, as, for instance, it often happens that a most insignificant piece of music attains a good result in consequence of the beautiful words to which it is set; really good music, of course, in such a case will all the more produce a heightened effect.

If we now first turn once more to the characteristic formation of music with reference to a proposed object, we remember that above (1) we had to reject altogether the question as to an object of music in general. We had to state that the practice of musical art, like that of any other art, is, in the first instance, a manifestation of impulses common to all men, — of the impulse of communication and the impulse of playing. "Out of the abundance of the heart the mouth speaketh". Joy and grief man is not prone to keep to himself. "Imparted joy is double joy, imparted pain, reduced by half." If man abandons himself to his natural impulse, he will, like the child or the savage, shout and leap for joy, weep and shudder with pain. Thus music and dance, at least, are the direct outcome of strongly aroused sentiment and of the impulse to communicate, which, as is well known, in default of sympathetic reasonable persons, directs itself towards the unreasoning creation, the animal and plant world, even towards the lifeless inorganic world, towards anything visible or tangible. The child talks not only to its dolls, but also to the chairs, tables, plates, and tells them its grief as well as its joy.

The impulse to *play*, then, gives to the manner of communication its special form by trying to put everything in an easily comprehensible order, that is, by composing parts to a whole, showing the parts in symmetrical relation, — in a word, by consistency. Thus the joyful jumping becomes dance by keeping to certain movements and repeating them periodically; thus, too, the joyful shouting becomes a well ordered combination of tones, — a melody. Poetry, in a manner just as clear, shows the same elements: the communication of sentiment by means of words (pure lyric poetry), and the ordering of the form of the communication in the shape of measured verses with or without rhyme (metre).

It is the manifestation of another impulse that gives rise to the imitative arts, namely the impulse to *imitate*, the desire to copy something existing outside of us, something complete in itself, instead of what manifests itself in the action of the impulse to play, namely imitation during the making, that is, development of a motive. Architecture shows a decided amalgamation of the two forms of imitation; it imitates nature by borrowing its pillars and buttresses from the forms of the trees, its vaults from the sky, etc.; but it also imitates — though again in copying nature — in the smaller and smallest details, its own formations during the process of forming, that is to say, it develops motives. Painting and sculpture appear still more dependent on the imitation of something existing as a complete thing, in as far as they copy figures and landscapes of the visible world or reproduce them from memory, — though they, too, like the other arts, may create with some freedom, combining the elements in a varying fashion, in which, indeed, an imitation of the smallest forms cannot be so clearly recognised, but at all events a symmetrical grouping can be observed, such as pyramidal arrangement, pleasant shading of tints, or something similar. Poetry and music likewise can widen their sphere by imitation of the world of phenomena; poetry by description, that is to say, by awakening, through the help of words, mental images corresponding to reality; music by imitation of the audible, by copying the forms of movement of the visible, and especially by the substitution of different timbre or pitch for effects of light and colour. Still the original forms of music as well as of poetry are those arising not from the impulse to imitate, but from the impulse to impart, — absolute music and pure poetry.

Considered in this way the essence of poetry, music, and dance (pantomime), appear as a going out of oneself, as it were, as an objectivation of the subject; and the essence of the imitative arts, on the other hand, as arising from the desire to make our own what is outside of us, to draw it into ourselves, therefore as a subjectivation of the object. Descriptive poetry and pictorial music give to the object itself life and voice, place the subject in the object, so that the work of art appears as life manifestation not of the artist, but of the persons or natural forces, scenes, landscapes, etc., imagined by him. Thus it is not Franz Liszt who imparts himself to us in longing grief and afterwards in proud exultation of artistic triumph, when we hear *Tasso lamento e trionfo*, but Tasso himself, as he lives in Liszt's imagination. And similarly in the second movement of his "Pastoral" symphony, it is not Beethoven who depicts for us his feelings as he gazes on the brook meandering through green meadows with its overshadowing trees, and on the feathered singers that hop among the branches and on the ground — rather there are painted the life manifestations of the landscape itself, which Beethoven experienced in his heart and which he, in the second instance, makes us experience with him.

Imitative music and descriptive poetry, therefore, like painting and sculpture, are the objectivations of subjectivated objects, while lyric poetry and absolute music are objectivations of the subject itself. But this is to be understood only for the creating artist. The listener, looker on, or reader, has to subjectivate the work of art again: in music, therefore, what was a subjective feeling of the composer, but was secreted, so to speak, by him as a work of art, was objectivated — that the listener has again to experience as his own feeling, therefore to subjectivate again. In absolute music he has to do this not by placing himself in the stead of the composer, but with the full delusion of feeling himself what the author felt; in descriptive music, however, for instance in the Tasso Symphony, only in this way that he is sympathetically touched by Tasso or rather by this particular Tasso, and that with him he suffers and rejoices.

It is clear that in imitative music something intervenes between hearer and composer, namely the represented object, which the composer has subjectivated only again to objectivate it as artistic work.

This repeated subjectivation and objectivation sufficiently explains the contradiction in the distinction we have given above between subjective and objectivating music, and the common distinction badly according with it between subjective and objective composers, subjective and objective players or singers. For he plays objectively who does not subjectivate, absorb, his object, namely the work to be played, to such an extent that it is, as it were, newly created by him, and appears with true tokens of a new creation, namely fresh, throbbing warmth of life in the dynamic and agogic shadings, that it carries us away and warms us whether we will or not; but who rather, with a kind of cool reserve, avoids approaching the object closely, and in consequence only as it were copies with rule and compass the drawing before him.

An objective *composer* is he who does not so much give himself up passionately to his feelings while creating a work of art, but rather himself relishes with special delight the beautiful form his work takes; therefore the Classicist who never loses sight of the beautiful form, in contradistinction to the Romanticist who revels in sentiment.

Thus we see that there may be subjective composers who write objectivating music, even that just they who care less about beautiful form than about characteristic substance, can be in a position to create objects having all the notions of subjectivity, — objects, therefore, that appear as endowed with life in a higher degree than the conventional creations of a formalist into which no real blood is infused. In as much, therefore, as the more subjective composer can imagine himself more vividly in the place of the objective character to be represented, the latter will appear with all the more vitality and truth.

This more marked prominence of subjective feeling in composers who write objectivating music is probably by chance, it is rather a peculiarity of our art-epoch to be explained by other reasons, than a logical necessity. Accidentally the idea that a kind of music representing not the interior life of the composer, but that of any historic or mythical personage, or some action or a piece of nature, has a more intense effect, came to be accepted at a time when the subjective mode of writing, — that is to say that which favoured the elementary factors more than the form-giving principles — also developed more strongly, namely after Beethoven. But Beethoven himself furnishes the most striking proof that the more decided breaking through of the emotional element does by no means urge towards objectivating music. For Beethoven is greatest where he manifests his own individuality, and therein precisely the elementary overpowers the formal most. There can hardly be anything more mistaken than the attempt to furnish a programme of Beethoven's last quartets, sonatas, and symphonies, and to show what Beethoven might have intended to represent in them: they are purely subjective music, in which not even the formal — the only thing, as I pointed out above, that might be called objective in the subjective work of art — is finished to such perfection that it could fully accomplish that process of purifying and redeeming which the work of art is called to achieve in the artist's soul. It is similar with Brahms, with whom also often enough the "world's pain" peeps through, that is to say, art has not succeeded fully in sweetening, by the perfection of the formal, the pain from which the work of art sprang.*)

A peculiar physiognomy is shown by Schumann who loves to divide his fanciful natural disposition, which on the one side is meditative and dreamy, on the other strongly effervescing and impetuous, into its separate potentialities, and as it were to represent himself as the object with a more prominent or exclusive development of the one or the other side of his temperament. Thus he succeeded in creating a large number of pictures of mental dispositions of marvellous sharpness and characteristic distinction, which do not belong to imitative music, although they often have titles; nor properly to purely subjective music, because they have not the fluctuating, developing character of pure subjectivity, but are, as it were, instantaneous photographs of the subject made the object.

Purely subjective is Chopin who revels in the elementary as hardly any other musician; I say "revels", for a Beethoven and a Brahms do not revel in it, but the former struggles with the expression of the ideas stirring up his whole soul, and Brahms immerses himself in dark depths of human sentiment with a certain blissful awe, with the lust of pain, while Chopin abandons himself to a sweet dreaming, to an agreeable vision, a charming illusion, to which broad daylight would bring death. Chopin never objectivates, not even himself.

The two most exclusive masters of imitative music are Berlioz and Liszt, both fiery spirits and capable in an eminent degree of transferring themselves into the soul of another, therefore what we call truly subjective natures.

---

*) Arthur Seidl, in his recently published degree dissertation "Vom Musikalisch-Erhabenen", calls this remainder of the elementary which the formal has not been able to overcome, or rather this breaking of the elementary through the fetters of the formal, the "sublime in music". According to Seidl the ugly is "not yet beautiful", and the sublime, "no longer beautiful". I hereby emphatically call attention to this little book written with great industry and acute critical power, with which, unfortunately, I did not become acquainted until after my second lecture. Seidl in several places comes very near to the principle set up by myself, of subjectivating the work of art.

To prove this we need only point to Liszt's piano playing which, more than that of any other, always was new creation of the work.

What, then, are the means by which these associations of ideas are aroused of necessit y in our imagination, — these associations of ideas whose development renders possible the comprehension of the imitative musical work of art?

Up to this we have made only a few remarks about the characteristic effects of timbre or pitch, and of strength of tone; it is obvious that also the manner of movement, as rhythm and tempo, has to contribute essentially to producing the intended effects. All forms of movement that are to be imitated or somehow suggested to the imagination, are made clear in their course by means of *crescendo* and *diminuendo*, as well as *stringendo* and *ritardando;* they are placed into bold relief by dynamic and agogic shadings. All combinations of the elementary factors retain their peculiar effects even when we hear, not subjectively, but objectively, when we do not identify ourselves, but only sympathize; thus *diminuendo* towards the higher notes becomes a fleeting, evanescing, *crescendo* towards the deep notes, a powerful rush of great masses, the *pianissimo* of sustained or vibrating harmonies covering the whole compass of tone, a wide plain, be it of the calm, smooth ocean, or of the bare, burning desert, or perhaps the unmeasured space of the bright, starry nocturnal sky. Jagged or waved lines of all kinds, as the tone movement (melody) exhibits them, become directly the adequate expression of visible motions of a corresponding form.

Rhythm naturally gains prominent importance. Hopping, violent bouncing, soft clinging, running, stopping, and all the thousandfold graduated and intermixing possibilities, become as many easily intelligible manifestations of life and of the forms of movement of the represented object, if once we are directed to experience music not actively, that is, with the *will*, but as spectators, that is, with the *imagination.*

Which is to be placed higher, subjective or objectivating music? This question is better not put at all. If the same tone combinations can mean now a passionate emotion of the heart, at another time the galloping of a horse, or something else taken from the world of phenomena, it is idle to dispute about the superiority of the one or the other. This, indeed, seems to be quite unquestionable, that all objectivating music has a transferred, not an original, meaning, as can be sufficiently seen from the fact that in many cases without a knowledge of the programme little or nothing can be made of the music.

Under all circumstances, therefore, we are referred back to the characteristic property, that is to say, the agreement of the effect produced and the object proposed. We will add, first, a few words more about that general characteristic property mentioned above, according to which dance music, for instance, is not suitable during a funeral procession, as on the contrary it is impossible to trip a merry dance to a funeral march; or as noisy fanfares of trumpets and kettle-drums do not appear adapted to lull a child to sleep, while an army would hardly care to charge to the sounds of a gentle, insinuating melody. For divine service, — and here again differently according to the festivals of the ecclesiastical year, — for festive processions, for a burial service, for a serenade, etc., — in a word according to the special occasion that requires music, music must have a more or less pronounced character, or at least must not be altogether in contradiction to the required state of mind.

If we said that attention to a definite object itself deprives music of a part of the ideal artistic freedom, — a statement that must decidedly be adhered to, — we must not consider music of a special kind, suited for a particular case, as composed as a provision for emergencies, but as created out of the situation. It does not matter that this situation may have existed only in the imagination. Music of this kind need not have even a touch of objectivating meaning, but may be altogether subjective. We have to remark, however, that a march, dance, cavalry fanfare, or cradle-song, has each its own natural rhythm, which hardly can be called a means of artistic effect, but is rather a kind of vessel into which music is infused, a sort of fetter which it has to bear under the given circumstances, simply because we walk slowly in a funeral march and spring quickly in the Galop. It must not be overlooked, however, that everything else is not thereby directed into a special course; it is quite possible to make most merry, playful music within the general rhythm necessitated by the walking pace of the funeral march, while on the other hand the rhythm of the Galop might be distinctly marked, and still a strictly ecclesiastical stamp given to the whole by means of a *Cantus firmus* in long notes.

What regards Church music in particular, its conception, besides comprehending what is suited for the situation, namely, slow movement and dignified harmony, is frequently modified by something that can only be called historic characterisation, namely, that strange formation of harmony which, instead of the clarified modern tonality, favours the peculiar, not strained but straining turns of the so-called Church tones. If by that means a proposed object is more easily attained, for instance, in the opera or any other piece of imitative music, no objection can be raised to it. But it must be called entirely wrong, if a composer of our days whenever he wants to raise his voice fervently to his God, thinks himself obliged to use the dialect of a by-gone time.

Up to this moment, that is to say, to the end of our reflections, we have intentionally avoided *vocal music*, not as if we had shunned the discussion of its principles, but rather in order to let it be seen unambiguously that we do not need the reference to vocal music for the explanation of any principle of absolute music. For of absolute music, vocal music forms no part.

It is an old point of dispute; Which is the older, vocal music or instrumental music? This dispute, as a general rule, is decided in favour of vocal music; for as they say, the singing voice is the oldest, because the natural, musical instrument of man; instrumental music is taken as originating in vocal music, and laws for the former are derived from the latter. The most prominent representative of this one-sided view, which not only favours vocal music by preference, but even declares instrumental music to be an aberration, was Eduard Grell, Professor of the department of composition at the Berlin Academy, who died in August 1886. I may be permitted to quote here a few samples from his collected Treatises and Opinions on music, published after his death by Heinrich Bellermann, who, by the way, is of the same way of thinking. In the introduction Grell states his principle in a very plain and unmistakable way (page 3): "A musical idea comprises three things: 1. *Words*, 2. Harmony, 3. Rhythm, which are most intimately connected and exist simultaneously; of these three, the words not only supply the soul, the substance of the subject-matter, but they also give rise, by their vowels, to harmony (?), and, by their consonants, to rhythm (?)." On page 127 he says: "Music without words and ideas, that is instrumental music, would be sensuality that we abhor; it would correspond in painting to a mixture of figures and colours without subject-matter." Page 40: "To future times it will appear inexplicable that in our times singing was considered so low and unessential, instrumental music so high and important... For designing and painting without subject-matter, for instance patterns for clothes and tapestry [thus a Beethoven symphony = tapestry pattern!] are not easily advocated by anyone or considered as art. But the most intellectual people are charmed by the mixture, devoid of ideas, of merely rhythmic and harmonic relations, that is to say by instrumental music.. But this is an effect of an altogether sensuous nature, not in the remotest degree warranted or having a definite direction, an effect which no art is required to produce, but mere nature, the mere noise of nature, is sufficient and even capable of producing with more intensity and power." Finally on page 144: "Nature herself has led up to the art of raising speech to singing by the measurement of time and sounds — rhythm and harmony. Thus it appears that instrumental music is an extremely beautiful garment in which only the chief thing, namely the body, is wanting. Or we may say that it is a wonderfully beautiful body, but without soul, without idea, without word. (It is written: In the beginning was the Word!) From the explained genealogy it appears that of all instrumental music the sublimest is dance music. The dance is the rhythmical element, the metre, of poem and words. No instrumental music, therefore, comes as near to the expression of ideas as dance music. For although it cannot give the word, still it recalls it by retaining the scheme of the metre, of the verse and of its words. And as a matter of fact, what nowadays is considered as the highest degree of instrumental music, namely the symphony, is nothing else than dance music. The symphony, like the sonata . . . has originated in the so-called suites, that is to say, serieses of dances, which, because people ceased to dance to them, have so terribly degenerated that, when hearing modern symphonies, we can think no longer of dances, of dancing, or even of verses. The only pieces that sometimes are left are the Minuet and the March, and of these the Minuet in such a corrupted form that not even the three-four time is sure of its life. So far progress can lead. Instead of the various characteristic dance rhythms, nowadays in the symphony the wildest and most unintelligible rhythms are presented", and so forth. Page 145: "As soon as the musician makes the handicraft, the manufacturing of the product as it were, the main thing, the wordless implements come into activity. Then the idea flies away, and poetry is gone."

He who wrote this was for many years one of the most esteemed musical authorities for the highest administrative organs of the Prussian state! Hence it is well worth while to take note of the extreme narrowness of his standpoint.

The fundamental error of Grell, out of which everything else follows as a natural consequence, is the supposition that music has developed out of speech, the exact opposite of which, of course, must be true. Does singing really arise from a heightening of speech, or is speech, originally, perhaps only faded singing?

That the singing of the human voice is the "beautiful of nature" in music, or, better, the prototype of music, the criterion, the canon by which all aesthetic values of musical productions are measured, was the red thread that ran through our considerations. But this by no means proves that singing in connection with words, that is, the combination of music and poetry, forms the foundation of music. What are words? Words are nothing else than conventional symbols to designate concrete things or abstract notions. Naturally the conventional formulas for abstract notions are of much more recent origin than those for concrete things. It is well known that many words are so-called onomatopoetic imitations of the auditory or visual impressions made by the things or phenomena designated by them, for instance, rattling, creaking, whistling, glittering, etc. But generally the origin of language, which naturally cannot clearly be defined, has its last recognisable traces in crude utterances of joy and pain, of desire, detestation or anger, in a word, of affections, and it is to be understood in a similar way as the elementary factors of music, of which we have treated at length. Beyond all doubt these original utterances were the starting point for the development of language as well as of singing. But the word proper, as such, as symbol, not as expression of feeling that is generally intelligible and affects us in an elementary manner by the elementary effects of change of pitch, etc., but as formula fixed by conventional usage to designate a thing or a notion, a feeling, a desire, like heat or thirst, — is certainly not a development of primitive elements, but a fading and ossification of the original meaning of sounds, brought about by the development of other mental faculties, namely reason and memory, and under the influence of the impulse of communicating, for the purpose of a more manifold and at the same time more definite use. The original meaning of sounds, however, did not become forgotten or obsolete, but rather, without any doubt, simultaneously with the development of languages, became heightened to singing. But from that point word and singing diverge; from the moment when the word passes from the absolute meaning of its sound to the conventional and traditional, the tonic (vocalic) and rhythmic (which does not consist, as Grell indicates, in the consonants but merely in the weight of the syllables; the consonants only effect a smoother connection or varying sharp separation of the vowels), in a word, the musical, elements attaching to the word, become merely the means necessary for hearing, the material, as it were, of the words, while with their meaning they retain less and less connection. Still speech retains the capability of utilising these elementary means again in a higher degree according to their original meaning, and it does this in measured speech, from the melodic cadences of an elaborate oration up to the real declamation and recitation of a poem. The word cannot do without tone, and it does not fail to make use of it to greater extent for the highest gradation of its effect. We can certainly say with the same right that poetry desires the tone, that is, ordered combinations of tone, real music, as it has often been declared that (absolute) music desires the word. How rarely has anybody been tempted to compose words to a beautiful melody, although that would often enough be quite possible! But no verse capable of music is safe from being flooded again and again with music. Would that be intelligible if music with words were a gradation of music without words? But it is quite intelligible, because words with music are a gradation of words without music. And in what could the gradation of music without words to music with words consist? Apparently only in the reception of an altogether new element, not in the gradation of one contained in it already. For this new element would be the meaning which the word has, abstracting from its sound, the meaning given to it by convention and tradition, without its being warranted by its vocalic, consonantic, and rhythmic effect. It is different when music is added to the word, changing the speaking tone into singing. The task that then confronts the composer may be defined as consisting in his having to bring back language to its original condition, and to give back to its vowels, consonants, and rhythm the same significance which they must have had in the primitive utterances of sentiment. It is manifest that this task can be only partially fulfilled. Otherwise there would be, for each poem, only one melody, namely, that which alone would give the single words their true accentuation. But according to our explanation of the development of language, it is impossible that every word should find an equivalent in the musical expression, for the simple reason that a large number of words, especially abstract notions and auxiliary words, are formed in an altogether conventional manner, are merely the result of the protracted living together of men. Not the emphasising of the significance of the *single word*, therefore, can be the task of singing, but rather the expression of the meaning of the single thoughts. Only for these will it be possible to find, unless the idea be too abstract and devoid of every sentimental element, a really equivalent musical expression, and not only one, but many. Some influence on the formation of the melody, indeed, will be exerted by the single words, because, above all, their rhythmical element cannot be ignored without interfering with their intelligibility. The so-called correct declamation of the words in singing consists merely in the elaboration of the natural rhythm of the words, that is, of the different weight of the syllables. And this difference of treatment is not to be confined to the correct distinction of strong and weak in the single word, but, I am inclined to say, it is of still more importance regarding the syllables which require emphasis according to the sense, those on which the chief stress of the *sentence* falls.

This necessity of paying attention to the rhythm of language may have given rise to the error that singing generally is only a gradation of the natural cadence of the words, a view which, I think, I have refuted in my preceding observations. The natural cadence is the same in all sentences of equal construction, that is to say according as they are question or statement, command or request, and as they have subordinate sentences of this or that kind; and the greater or less number of words that may be used, is hardly of importance for anything but the *tempo*. The cadence of the single words requires special attention only when the meaning requires emphasis for them, that is, when they contain the main idea of the sentence. Then the musical formation, too, must culminate in them; but sufficient consideration is given if only the syllable that has the principal weight in the particular word has it also in the whole phrase or period. The proper musical structure of the melody, however, will depend on the sentiment which the words, or rather the sentences, express, and in this respect, as we know, the elementary factors will be of most importance. Compare, for instance, Mendelssohn's "Spring Song": "Es brechen in schallenden Reigen die Frühlingsstimmen los", and Schubert's "Du bist die Ruh, der Frieden mild!". The restlessly flickering melody of the former song, rushing quickly from depth to height, and taking a fresh start again and again, in its contrast to the quiet lines of the latter, that strive upwards with energy, indeed, but not quickly and jerkily, but in long-drawn strokes, forms a characteristic example of the effect of the elementary factors.

While thus, indeed, song music is eminently adapted to be heard subjectively, that is to say, with the full delusion of personal experience, because singing is the manner peculiar to us of giving audible expression to our feelings, still we must not overlook that for the composer the case is essentially different. If the composer is not also the poet, and even in that case, if the words are there completed, and the music is not composed simultaneously with the words but afterwards, (what, as we know, even with Wagner was always the case), then the music to be invented belongs to the objectivating class; for the composer cannot let his imagination work freely, but is bound to the musical illustration of the text before him; he, therefore, can make mistakes which would be impossible if he were to create quite unhindered, from within himself. He can mistake the character of the whole, he can fail to bring out sufficiently some main features of the poem, he even can sin, by a contradiction of the expression of the music and the meaning of the words, to such an extent that the effect is altogether ridiculous, however correct and pleasing the music separated from the words may be. It is a bad sign, of course, for the quality of his artistic power, if such a thing happens to him.

The converse, the case that the music well agrees with the expression of the words, but without them has no real musical meaning, is also unpleasant enough, but at least not ridiculous. Only where the subject-matter of the words is sufficient compensation for the loss of musical effect, such a formation can be considered as warranted; so, for instance, in the often long spun out secco-recitatives of the older operas, in which the musical interest is almost equal to zero, while, in compensation, the action advances more quickly, and also a foil is gained by which subsequent numbers constructed on purely musical lines are set off to better advantage. The modern opera dispenses with this kind of recitative, which is hardly heightened speech, but only speech on a definite pitch, and to which recourse is had in order to prevent the glaring contrast of the key of the instruments and the pitch of the declaimer, which is so disagreeably felt in the melodrama. Instead of this, the modern opera uses the accompanied recitative, that is to say, the voice, indeed, speaks more than it sings, but the purely musical interest is satisfied by the thematic formations displayed in the accompaniment. This kind of singing, which is developed to the highest perfection especially by Wagner, is, indeed, only heightened speech, but for that same reason not real singing. The real singing takes place whenever not the single word, but the meaning of the phrases and sentences, finds its musical expression, whether a transition is made to the formal structure of song on a large scale, that is to the *aria*, or whether only a few bars assume an *arioso* character.*)

The relation of the accompaniment to the singing voice can be of a very varying kind. If the thematic structure is in the song, if, therefore, we have real singing before us, the accompaniment may confine itself to explaining the melody of the voice in its harmonic struc-

---

*) Strangely G. Engel (Aesthetik, p. 115) asks: "Who can know whether, while he wrote a vocal composition, the melody invented floated before the mind of the composer as a purely melodic formation, or influenced by the incitement and reflection of the words for which he invented it?" Can a worse reproach be made to a composer than that he had invented the melody of a vocal composition without reference to, without being influenced by, the words? Apparently Engel has overlooked that the possibility of melody formation in connection with words is of a two-fold kind: in broad outlines, and in detail. The singer, however, (with whom Engel is concerned primarily) will in any case have a good deal of work left for him to do; it will be easiest for him to bring out the meaning of the words when the composer has worked in detail. But where the melody expresses the feeling in great outlines, he certainly must have enjoyed some "style-culture", if he is to be able to let the meaning of the words appear clearly as light undulations on the surface of the deeper waves of the general emotion. Very appropriately Richard Wallaschek remarks in his "Aesthetik der Tonkunst" (1886) that things which, in a prosaic description, would be quite in their place, easily receive from music a tone of solemnity which would create general laughter if the regard for the composer or the place of the performance did not preclude such a thing; (p. 345) "when the evangelist (in Bach's 'Passion according to St. Matthew') announces in the most solemn Andante, with the accompaniment of long-drawn chords .... with most serious voice: 'now the coat was without seam, woven from the top throughout' etc." These are cases where the composer, if he cannot avoid the composition of such words, must confine himself to fixing the cadence and rhythm of the words, because a musical interpretation of the meaning is impossible. By the way, Wallaschek's book is one of the most barren and unpleasant that have appeared for a long time on the field of musical aesthetics. One sentence may suffice to characterise it (p. 205): "The human voice could not then serve as a regulator because it was too uncertain as long as one could not learn, from instruments (!), the strict limitation aud invariable pitch of the tone". This passage is a nice pendant to Grell's views on instrumental music!

ture, and thereby to supporting and strengthening its effect; or it may participate in the thematic treatment by imitating parts of the vocal melody, in which case it combines more intimately with the voice part, but also easily runs the risk of making itself intrusively prominent; third, the accompaniment may illustrate, in an independent manner, the meaning of the words. This latter case requires a little more attention. We have to distinguish again several methods of treatment. The accompaniment may confine itself to maintaining the general expression of the text, which does not exclude its painting, for instance, the whispering of the evening breeze, or the rippling of the brook, or the roaring of the storm. It will be the business of the singing voice, then, to express sharply the different features, the varying phases of feeling, which the words suggest. But also, on the contrary, the singing voice can undertake to draw the general outlines, to maintain the general sentiment, while the accompaniment goes into detail, particularises, illustrates the meaning of each line of poetry. In the larger forms of vocal music, namely the opera and the oratorio, several other combinations are possible; for instance, the accompaniment may carry on the action, or at least portray, by objectivating independently, and not in connection with the meaning of the words, of the singing voice. Or the accompanying music may betray the most secret thoughts, while the singing conceals them; it is possible for the accompaniment to give a processional march or something of the kind, while one or more singing voices express themselves subjectively. Think also, for instance, of the first scene of the "Meistersinger" (in the Church), where, during the singing of the chorale, the solo parts of the orchestra (violin, 'cello, oboe) interpret the love dialogue of Walther and Eva who talk in silent signs.

It is not my intention to indicate here all the possibilities of distributing the parts, much less to explain them in detail. We had only to state generally how music and word in vocal music are related to each other, and to get a clear understanding whether vocal music is really the Alpha and Omega of music, or only one of its forms. I think we cannot remain doubtful on this point. Vocal music is not "music simply", but a combination of music with poetry, in the opera with acting also, made for the purpose of mutual support, of working in concert, of attaining artistic effects of the very highest intensity.

I will not conclude my paper without acknowledging tha in the musical drama effects are possible that neither music alone, nor poetry alone or in combination with acting, could produce. The illusion of real occurrence is certainly effected most perfectly by the acting; in the word the acting persons express their thinking and feeling unambiguously, and whatever may be wanting, music supplies by raising the expression high above the mere conventional, and by making the meaning of the words much more intelligible and forcible through its direct action on the feelings. But it is not men alone who speak this sublime language; even nature speaks to us directly through the voice of the orchestra.

If now, looking back, we ask ourselves how the listener acts with reference to the various kinds of music that we considered, we must again and again put the greatest stress on this, that absolute music, pure instrumental music as well as vocal music connected with pure lyric poetry, must be subjectivated with the full delusion of personal experience; but that also objectivating music, — the illustrating, accompanying music of the song, of the opera, of the pantomine, and of the melodrama, as well as the independent programme-music — can produce its full effect only when the listener succeeds in bringing himself into sympathetic contact with the object. Thus even when music actually paints nature, be it in storm or in peaceful idyllic repose, he must try to transport himself in imagination into the life-conditions of the objects which the music is to represent.

But the activity of the mind is essentially different with objectivating music and with purely subjective music. For with the latter only a sharp comprehension of the passing tone-pictures, a retention in the memory and a comparison, an attention to the symmetric formations and proportions, therefore, at all events, a pleasureable enjoyment of what is offered, is required. With imitative music, however, it is necessary to understand in detail the intentions of the composer, by making one's imagination work on in the direction suggested by the composer. Nobody will deny that, in certain circumstances, this is a very precarious thing. For when the word does not accompany us as a safe guide, and give to the ambiguous formations of music their special meaning, it cannot but happen occasionally that the imagination of the listener runs away with him, and, through a misunderstanding of the intention of the composer due not to a culpable want of judgment, but explainable by the ambiguity of the music, he completely loses the thread of the programme. This is the reason why all protracted programmes, in which an action develops itself, become more or less impracticable, not for the composer but for the listener.*) I remember a striking example, namely the orchestral piece "Don Quixote" by Rubinstein. With the programme in my hand I was not able to follow the thread, but imagined at different places that the moment had come, when the gallant knight fights against a flock of sheep. Where the word keeps the mind *au courant*, bridles and spurs the imagination, the capability of music is unlimited; also where the programme only indicates, with a few words, the *situation* (not a developing action), music is capable of the highest effect. I recall, for instance, Liszt's ingenious piano tone-picture "St. Francis of Paula walking on the waves", which has an unsurpassibly plastic effect.

The attempt of the founder of modern programme music, Hector Berlioz, to give to the dissolving form of the tone-picture a stronger skeleton by means of retaining and transforming a few motives, must be recognised as very ingenious, but will hardly ever attain great results; for even the leading-motive will lead safely only where the word is at hand: there it can, as we know from Wagner's works, enforce the most significant associations of ideas with unfailing certainty. The recurrence of a

---

*) A little too sharp, indeed, but otherwise concurring in this view is G. Engel's judgment (Aesthetik, p. 53): "The most exhaustive programme cannot afford a full compensation for the want of musical unity, because the poetic meaning is not imminent in the composition, bar by bar, tone by tone, by means of the word, as in vocal music. But since this is so, an *exhaustive* programme is of no particular value; for it deflects the attention of the listener from the piece of music, that, to be understood in its unity, demands this attention in the fullest measure. Programme music, therefore, is a superfluous hybrid," etc.

motive, emphatically announced for the first time in a situation of special importance, will each time recall this situation to the memory; the best instance of this continues to be the "Never shalt thou question me" in Lohengrin. But whether the extended use of the motives, as carried out by Wagner in his latest music dramas, must not ossify, in the hands of less ingenious composers, to a dry conventionalism of the very worst kind, the future alone will decide.

In any case, I think, the consideration of the various means by which music produces its artistic effects, has afforded us no ground whatever to attribute less value to the works of any of our Classics or Romanticists than to those of any other. Rather all appear, notwithstanding all intended and more or less successful objectivations, as reflected images of great individual artists; and the thought that we can feel ourselves at one with them for minutes, elevates and strengthens our minds. And so we shall not slight any one form of art in favour of another, nor allow either pure instrumental music, in which the subjective sentiment expresses itself most directly, to be depreciated, or vocal music, which, with the assistance of the word, is capable of leading the mind to the most sublime conceptions, to be treated with less respect.

For EU product safety concerns, contact us at Calle de José Abascal, 56–1°,
28003 Madrid, Spain or eugpsr@cambridge.org.

www.ingramcontent.com/pod-product-compliance
Ingram Content Group UK Ltd.
Pitfield, Milton Keynes, MK11 3LW, UK
UKHW041948230426
12048UKWH00008B/207